# IELTS

# Preparation and Practice

## Listening and Speaking

Wendy Sahanaya and Jeremy Lindeck

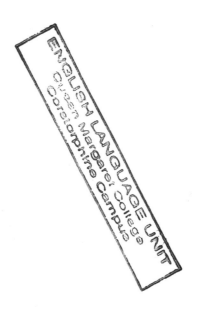

Melbourne

OXFORD UNIVERSITY PRESS

# OXFORD
UNIVERSITY PRESS

Oxford
ANZ
English

253 Normanby Road, South Melbourne, Australia

Oxford University Press is a department of the University of Oxford.
It furthers the University's objective of excellence in research, scholarship,
and education by publishing worldwide in

Oxford  New York

Athens  Auckland  Bangkok  Bogotá  Buenos Aires  Calcutta
Cape Town  Chennai  Dar es Salaam  Delhi  Florence  Hong Kong  Istanbul
Karachi  Kuala Lumpur  Madrid  Melbourne  Mexico City  Mumbai  Nairobi
Paris  Port Moresby  São Paulo  Singapore  Taipei  Tokyo  Toronto  Warsaw

with associated companies in Berlin  Ibadan

OXFORD is a registered trade mark of Oxford University Press
in the UK and in certain other countries

© Wendy Sahanaya, Jeremy Lindeck 1997

First published 1997

Reprinted 1999

National Library of Australia
Cataloguing-in-Publication data:

Sahanaya, Wendy, 1940–.
  IELTS preparation and practice: listening and speaking.

  ISBN  0 19 554095 6.

  1. English language — Examinations. 2. International English Language Testing System.
  3. English language — Examinations, questions, etc. I. Lindeck, Jeremy, 1961–. II. Title.
  III. Title: International English Language Testing System preparation and practice.
  (Series: IELTS preparation and practice).

428

Edited by Eliza Collins
Cover and text design by Rob Cowpe Design
Illustrations by Juli Kent
Typeset by Banshee Graphics
Printed through Bookpac Production Services, Singapore

# Contents

# Preface

## How To Use This Book

In this practice book you will work your way through a Practice Listening test from beginning to end. You will need to work with the book and the audio cassette together.

When you see the words **START YOUR TAPE NOW** in the book, you should start the cassette tape and follow the instructions given in both the book and on the tape. You must start your cassette tape at this point in order to do the exercises that follow.

When you hear and see the words **STOP YOUR TAPE** you should stop the cassette tape and work through the explanations and exercises in the book until you see **START YOUR TAPE NOW** again.

The first part of the book works through a Practice test, section by section, following the structure of a typical IELTS Listening test. The structure of each section is discussed and the type of questions demonstrated. Strategies are suggested for dealing with the various question types as well as for the Listening test in general. The recording for this is on Cassette 1 Side A.

**START YOUR TAPE NOW**

Listen to the instructions that appear on the front of the Listening test booklet.

When you hear the words *"now turn to Section one on page two of your question booklet"*

**STOP YOUR TAPE**

**DO NOT REWIND YOUR TAPE**

# The Listening Test

## About The Listening Test

All candidates taking the IELTS Test do the same type of Listening test, but the version differs according to the test date.

The Listening test takes about 30 minutes, with 10 minutes allocated for you to transfer your answers from the question booklet to the answer sheet.

The test is in four sections. Each section is more difficult than the one before. Sections one and two—*social situations*—are about everyday events, such as conversations about accommodation or shopping, or short talks giving practical information for daily living. Sections three and four—*course-related situations*—are about the typical situations students face in their courses of study, such as discussions with tutors or administrators and short, introductory course lectures.

### The Day of the Test

On the day of the test you will do the Listening section first. The examiner will:
- give you an answer sheet for the Listening and the Reading tests (see example on page 97)
- read you the general instructions for the whole test
- give you your IELTS Listening test booklet.

### The Test Format

- The test is recorded on a cassette tape.
- You hear the tape **once only**.
- First, the voice on the cassette tape reads the instructions on the front of the question booklet.

- **Read these instructions as you listen to the tape** to become accustomed to the speed and accent of the speech.
- You can ask the administrator to adjust the volume, if necessary.
- Do not open your booklet until you are told to do so.
- During the test you are given time to read the questions and to check back over your answers. **It is very important that you read these questions during this time.**
- You must answer the questions while you are listening.
- There are between 38 and 42 questions.
- The questions mostly follow the same sequence as the information contained in the Listening cassette.
- Write your answers to the questions directly into the question booklet.
- At the end of each section you will be given some time to go back and make sure your answers are clear.
- At the end of the test you have 10 minutes to transfer all your answers to the answer sheet.
- The tape will tell you when to stop writing.

There is a variety of possible question types. They are as follows:

- multiple choice
- short answers (up to three words)
- sentence completion (no more than three words)
- completing notes, a table or a summary
- labelling a diagram
- matching (e.g. pictures with what you hear).

You will be able to familiarise yourself with all of these kinds of questions as you work through this book.

## Getting the Instructions Right

**Note:** There are no exercises on the cassette tape for the following questions.

The written instructions in the Listening booklet are always given in *italics*. Important aspects of the instructions are also in ***BOLD ITALIC CAPITALS***.

The instructions in the Listening test depend on the type of question. If you familiarise yourself with the various types of instructions before the test you will be more likely to follow them properly. Time spent on familiarising yourself with instructions now, as you work through this book, means that you will be able to tell at a glance what you have to do in the actual IELTS Test. You will be less likely to make the more common mistakes.

### EXERCISE

The following instructions are typical of those you will find in the IELTS Listening booklet. Read each of the instructions and questions. Look at what the candidate did in both the Listening question booklet and on the answer sheet on page 5. Then say whether the candidate answered the questions appropriately or not.

*Circle the correct letter **A–D** for each question.*

**1**  What is Jane pleased about?

    **A**  meeting Steve         **B**  her holiday

    **(C)**  the semester finishing     **D**  her exam results

*Circle **TWO** letters **A–E**.*

**5**  What activities are they planning?

    **A**  camping         **(B)**  swimming

    **(C)**  cycling         **D**  hunting

    **E**  walking

*Label the diagram. Write the correct letters **A–E** next to the list of places.*

**8** bus depot             ......A.......

**9** sports stadium        ......D.......

**10** university           ......E.......

| A | | RAILWAY STATION |
|---|---|---|

| B | C | D | E |
|---|---|---|---|

*Complete the notes below. Write **NO MORE THAN THREE WORDS** for each answer.*

A complete degree requires **(16)** ...*72*... credit points. The form of assessment may be written, as in **(17)**... ***essays, exams, journals...***, or oral, as in seminars, or **(18)**... ***class participation*** ..., as in language courses.

*Copy the letter for the area of the map (**A–F**) and the activity against 25 and 26 in any order.*

**25  F  bird-watching**

**26  E  swimming**

*Complete the table with information about job applicants.*
*(Note: **X** means information not given.)*

| Name | Marital status | Age | Present job |
|------|----------------|-----|-------------|
| Max | *(31) ..single......* | X | technician |
| Marlene | X | 22 | *(32)..accountant...* |
| Jennifer | married | *(33)...27.........* | librarian |

What does Jo think about each assignment?

| *Write* | ✓ ✓ ✓ | *very difficult* |
|---------|-------|------------------|
|         | ✓ ✓   | *moderate*       |
|         | ✓     | *easy*           |

**37**  short essay          ....✓ ✓ ✓....

**38**  short film script     ........✓........

**39**  film review           .....✓ ✓.......

# Listening Answer Sheet

This is what the candidate wrote on the answer sheet. Check the instructions for each question and decide whether the candidate would be marked right or wrong. Indicate what you think by putting ✓ for right or ✗ for wrong in the right-hand column.

| | | |
|---|---|---|
| 1 | the semester finishing | |
| 2 | | |
| 3 | | |
| 4 | | |
| 5 | cycling, swimming | |
| 6 | | |
| 7 | | |
| 8 | A | |
| 9 | D | |
| 10 | university | |
| 11 | | |
| 12 | | |
| 13 | | |
| 14 | | |
| 15 | | |
| 16 | seventy-two | |
| 17 | essays, exams, journals | |
| 18 | participating in language classes | |
| 19 | | |
| 20 | | |
| 21 | | |
| | | |

| | | |
|---|---|---|
| 22 | | |
| 23 | | |
| 24 | | |
| 25 | F bird-watching | |
| 26 | swimming | |
| 27 | | |
| 28 | | |
| 29 | | |
| 30 | | |
| 31 | not married | |
| 32 | accountant | |
| 33 | 22 | |
| 34 | | |
| 35 | | |
| 36 | | |
| 37 | very difficult | |
| 38 | easy | |
| 39 | moderate | |
| 40 | | |
| 41 | | |
| 42 | | |
| Listening total | | |

Check your answers with the analysis given on the next page.

# Analysis of Candidate's Answers

**Question 1** The candidate circled the letter correctly in the booklet, but then transferred the full answer to the answer sheet. The candidate should have written only the letter **C** on the answer sheet. The answer would probably still be scored as correct, but it takes a lot longer to write than just the letter **C**.

**Question 5** The same as for question 1 above. This time the candidate should have written the two letters **C** and **B** on the answer sheet.

**Questions 8–9** These have been answered and transferred correctly.

**Question 10** The candidate wrote the word **university** instead of the letter **E**. There are no marks for just copying the information already provided in the question booklet.

**Question 16** This was answered and transferred correctly. For numbers it doesn't matter whether you write the number as a numeral or as words. However, the candidate has wasted time as it takes longer to write the words **seventy-two** than the numeral **72**.

**Question 17** This was answered and transferred correctly.

**Question 18** The candidate answered this one correctly in the Listening question booklet, then wrote **4** words on the answer sheet. This would be scored as wrong. When the instructions state **NO MORE THAN THREE WORDS**, four words is wrong.

**Question 25** This has been transferred correctly.

**Question 26** The candidate transferred the activity, but forgot to transfer the letter for the area. This would be marked wrong, as both the area and the activity need to be written in order to show that the candidate has truly understood what was said.

**Question 31** This has been transferred correctly. **Not married** means the same as **single**, but it takes longer to write.

**Question 32** This has been transferred correctly.

**Question 33** The candidate has transferred information from the wrong row of the table. You must be very careful not to do this in the exam.

**Questions 37–39** These have all been transferred incorrectly. The answers should be in the form of ticks or check marks (✓), not the items they refer to. These answers would probably still be scored as correct, but they take longer to write.

Now turn to page 7 of this book to start working your way through a Practice Listening test.

# The Listening Test
# Section 1

## What is it?

- It is a conversation, generally between two speakers.
- It is usually divided into two parts.
- First, you are given a little time (no more than 30 seconds) to look at the questions for Section 1.
- Then, you will hear an example.
- After the example, you will hear the correct answer.
- You will then have a little more time (about 20–30 seconds) to look at the questions for the first part of Section 1.

## The Example

Listening to the example gives you the chance to become familiar with the voices of the two speakers and to practise working out the answer **as you listen**.

Here is an example for you to practise. Read these instructions and the example as you listen to the tape.

### RE-START YOUR TAPE NOW

You will hear two friends talking about a trip they plan to take.

First, look at the example.

*Example*:  What is Jane pleased about?

    **A**   meeting Steve      **B**   her holiday

    **C**   the semester ending      **D**   her exam results

You will now hear the tape explain why **C** is the correct answer.

After you have heard this explanation

### STOP YOUR TAPE

## The Questions

### THE MAIN STRATEGIES ARE:

- reading **all** the questions in the section
- quickly analysing any answer choices.

You **must** study the questions and the answer choices during the time given for this activity. If you do not do this, you will not know what kind of information you should be listening for and you will not be ready to write your answers.

**REMEMBER, YOU MUST WRITE YOUR ANSWERS AS YOU LISTEN**

Although you are given time at the end of each section to check your answers, you will not be able to remember all of the information necessary to answer all the questions.

---

### T E S T   T I P S

- Become familiar with the instructions before you do the test.
- Practise listening as much as possible before you do the test.
- Listen carefully to the introduction to the test.
- Listen carefully to any instructions on the cassette.
- Write as much as you want in the question booklet.
- Write notes and answers directly into the question booklet **as you listen.**

---

Before continuing, you will need to start your cassette tape. During the time you are given to look at questions 1–7, quickly scan those questions and any answer choices. Try to analyse the kinds of information you will need to answer them. **Do not stop your tape to gain more time.** If you stop your tape, you will not be getting useful practice for the real test.

**NOW START YOUR TAPE**

and play it until you hear *"Because you have already heard the example, it is not repeated here."*

## SECTION 1  *Questions 1–11*

*Questions 1–7*

*Circle the correct answer.*

**1**   What does Jane plan to do during the break?

    **A**   fly home to stay with her family

    **B**   take summer courses

    **C**   take an overseas holiday

    **D**   go on a camping trip

**2**   Why can't Steve go home during the break?

    **A**   he has to earn some money to pay his fees

    **B**   he can't afford it

    **C**   he is taking a summer course

    **D**   he wants to study for next semester

**3** Where will Jane and her friends go during the semester break?

  **A** to Royal Island Park

  **B** to the mountains

  **C** to Royal National Park

  **D** to Great Southern Park

**4** Which route will the train follow?

  **A** Central, Sutherland, Garie

  **B** Sutherland, Caringbah, Waterfall

  **C** Central, Waterfall, Sutherland, Garie

  **D** Central, Sutherland, Waterfall

*Questions 5 and 6*

*Circle **TWO** letters for each answer.*

**5** Which of the following does Jane suggest Steve should bring?

| | | | |
|---|---|---|---|
| **A** | diving gear | **B** | cooking equipment |
| **C** | swimsuits | **D** | a sleeping bag |
| **E** | plenty of food | **F** | his bicycle |

**6** What activities are they planning?

| | | | |
|---|---|---|---|
| **A** | boating | **B** | scuba diving |
| **C** | bungee jumping | **D** | horse riding |
| **E** | hiking | **F** | surfboard riding |

*Question 7*

*Write a **NUMBER** for the answer.*

**7** If Steve joins them, how many people will be going on the trip?

_____

When you hear the words *"Now listen carefully and answer questions 1–7."*

**STOP YOUR TAPE**

## How to Answer—Demonstration

### ALL QUESTIONS

Write the answers to all questions directly into the question booklet. At the end of the test transfer the answers onto an answer sheet. There is a sample answer sheet on page 97 at the end of this book. Copy it. When you have completed all the sections of this Practice test, transfer the answers onto the answer sheet. Give yourself 10 minutes to do this.

## STEP 1—OVERVIEW OF THE INSTRUCTIONS

There are two types of instructions given in the examples. You are required to either circle the letters or write a number.

For questions 1–4 circle **one** answer, and for questions 5 and 6 circle **two** answers. You should circle the **letters** for the answers, not the **words** to ensure that you transfer your answers to the answer sheet correctly.

For question 7 you have to write a number. It does not matter whether you write the number as a numeral or as a word. So if the answer were 5, for example, either **5** or **five** would be acceptable.

## STEP 2—READ THE QUESTIONS AND THE ANSWER CHOICES

**What you can expect to hear**

The introduction to this section tells you that you are going to hear a conversation between two friends who are planning a holiday. You can expect to hear plans for the future and discussion about the type of trip. You might also hear them talking about what they will do on the trip.

A quick look at the questions tells you that you will be listening for specific information in each case, and you can expect to hear most of the words, or other words with the same meaning, in the answer choices for each question.

**What you have to do**

You have to decide as you listen how the answer choices relate to the question and what you hear. To help you do this, underline the **key words**; that is, the words that give you most information about what the answer will be.

For questions 1–4 the key words are highlighted as follows.

1   <u>What</u> does <u>Jane</u> plan to <u>do</u> during the break?

The question is about *an activity* that Jane (not Steve) will do.

All the answer choices give possible activities so you need to listen carefully for the one that Jane will do. You can expect to hear more than one of the answer choices mentioned, and you will have to decide whether it is Jane or Steve who plans to do each activity. You will also need to listen carefully to work out whether any of the activities might have been considered by Jane, but rejected for some reason.

2   <u>Why can't Steve go home</u> during the break?

'Why' tells you to listen for a *reason*. The question relates to Steve not Jane, and the reason relates to why he can *not* go home.

All the answer choices are reasons a student might not go home during the break. You might expect to hear more than one mentioned. It is also possible that the words spoken on the cassette tape will be different to those in the answer choices, so do not wait for the exact words you see in the booklet. There is a note on this point on page 12. You will also have to listen carefully to hear whether it is Jane or Steve who mentions the reason. You might hear Steve reject some of the reasons too.

**3** <u>Where</u> will Jane and her friends <u>go</u> during the semester break?

'Where' tells you to listen for a place, and you know from the introduction that the friends are planning a trip. This reveals a little about the kind of place they want to visit.

**4** <u>Which route</u> will the <u>train</u> follow?

The answer choices give you four possible routes. All you need to listen for is the correct sequence. As you listen it will be a good idea to number each station.

For questions 5 and 6 the instructions tell you to circle **TWO** letters for each answer. This means there are only two correct answers and you will have to get them both right to score **ONE** point for each question.
Look at question 5 and the answer choices.

**5** <u>Which</u> of the following does Jane suggest <u>Steve should bring</u>?

You need to notice that the answer choices are all *items possibly needed on a camping trip*. You will have to listen carefully for whether each item is mentioned or not, and when an item is mentioned, whether it is an item Steve should bring or not.

**6** <u>What activities</u> are they planning?

This is very similar to question 5 in that you will have to listen carefully to hear whether the activities are mentioned or not, and when they are mentioned, whether the group plans to do those activities or not. You could also think about whether you can eliminate any unlikely activities.

**7** <u>If Steve joins them, how many people</u> will be going on the trip?

The words 'how many people' tell you this question requires a number for the answer. You can write your answer either as a numeral or as a word. You are still listening for specific information. However, the beginning of the question has the words 'If Steve joins them'. These words tell you that you might expect to hear the number of people going without Steve, in which case you will have to add one.

Now turn back to pages 8 and 9

**START YOUR TAPE**

and try to answer questions 1–7, then

**STOP YOUR TAPE**

when you hear the instruction to do so.

**Note on question 2**

As you listened to the cassette tape you heard Steve say *"I don't really have enough money to fly home"*. Answer choice **B** ('he can't afford it'), means the same as what Steve says, so **B** is the correct answer. Answer choices in the booklet are often synonyms for the words you hear, as in this example.

You can check the rest of your answers with the key to this section in the Appendix (see page 94). If you still have difficulty with the answers, rewind your tape and listen to the section again.

**You should only check with the transcript if you can not get the answers in any other way.**

The cassette tape will now go on to the instructions for the next stage of Section 1. First, you will be told to look at the remaining questions in this section, which is a continuation of the dialogue. There is usually no further example for this stage.

In this Practice test you will need to match the areas given on a map with the activities the group expect to do in those areas.

**START YOUR TAPE NOW**

Listen to the instructions for this stage, and study questions 8–11.

*Questions 8–11*

*Label the areas of the map to show the activities the group will do in each. There are more activities than you will need.*

***Note:*** *Jane does not mention all of the areas. You will have to leave some blank.*

**List of activities**

rock climbing

swimming

cycling

cliff walks

boating

hunting

horse riding

scuba diving

bird-watching

*Copy the letter for the area of the map (A–F) and the activity against 8 to 11 in any order.*

**Questions 8–11**

   **8** ................

   **9** ................

 **10** ................

 **11** ................

**STOP YOUR TAPE**

## How to Answer—Demonstration

### STEP 1—OVERVIEW OF THE INSTRUCTIONS

Notice that there are no separate written questions here, just a list of activities and a map. The instructions tell you what to do with these. Not every Listening test has this type of activity, but it is important for you to familiarise yourself thoroughly with instructions of this type, so that you will not find them confusing during an actual test. First, you must write the activities on the map as you listen to the test. Although there is a line to write on for each area, the instruction tells you that you will not write on every line, as Jane does not mention every area. After that, you will have to **copy the LETTER for the area and the ACTIVITY against the numbers 8–11 IN ANY ORDER**. This does **not** mean you can put any activity with any map letter. It means that you can put **F swimming**, for example, against any of the numbers 8–11.

### STEP 2—READ THE QUESTIONS AND THE ANSWER CHOICES

**What you can expect to hear**
You can expect to hear the various areas of the park mentioned, usually by reference to the place names and directions in relation to those place names. When you see a map like this, think about the way people talk about directions and locations. Also, remember that north is always to the top of the page, unless there are compass points indicating otherwise. You can also expect to hear several of the activities. In fact, you might hear all of them mentioned.

**What you have to do**
You will notice that there are ten activities and six areas marked. However, there are only four questions. Therefore you know that you will not mark every area and you will not use every activity. So you must listen carefully for the activities the group plans to do, and *where* they can do them. You already know some of the activities they will do, based on the first part of the conversation, but you do not know in which area they will do them.

You can try to predict which activities are most likely. For example, you can predict that 'hunting' is unlikely, since they will be in a national park where it is usually forbidden to kill animals and birds or pick flowers. 'Horse riding' is also unlikely, as you know they will be going to the park by train. You cannot completely eliminate this of course—perhaps it will be possible to hire horses there.

## NOW START YOUR TAPE

Answer questions 8 to 11 as you listen. Mark your answers directly onto the map. When you have finished, stop your tape just after you hear the instruction to do so.

You will hear an instruction to copy your answers against questions 8–11 in any order. This means you copy your answers against numbers 8–11 in the Listening question booklet, **not** onto the answer sheet. It also means that it is only important to put the correct activity and the letter for the area together. So, for example, as long as **F** and **swimming** are together, it doesn't matter which number you write them beside.

## START YOUR TAPE

Mark your answers against the numbers.

When you hear the tape say *"That is the end of Section one. You now have half a minute to check your answers."*

## STOP YOUR TAPE

You will now be given half a minute to check your answers to Section 1. You should do this quickly, making sure that the answers are clear so that you will not have any trouble copying them onto your answer sheet later. If you have missed any questions, you can try to remember the answers now, though this is usually difficult to do. You can also try to guess any answers you failed to get, particularly for any multiple choice questions or matching questions.

If there is nothing further you can do with this section of the test, **go on and begin reading the instructions, questions and answer choices for the next section**. Do this for each section throughout the test.

## NOW START YOUR TAPE

Use the time appropriately, either to go over your answers or to read ahead, until you hear the instruction to turn to Section 2.

## STOP YOUR TAPE

### T E S T   T I P S

- Read all the instructions carefully.
- Read all the questions very quickly.
- Underline key words in the questions.
- Predict possible answers.
- Always write in a series of numbers while you are listening.
- Write notes and answers directly in the question booklet **as you listen**.

Now you can either practice predicting answers with the following exercises or go to Section 2 on page 17.

## *Prediction*

Sometimes it is possible to predict the likely answers to some of the questions in the IELTS Test before hearing the tape. This is one of the reasons why it is so important to spend as much time as possible looking at the questions before the tape is played.

In multiple choice questions, it is possible that at least one of the options is extremely unlikely. In such cases you can reduce the number of possible choices so you will have a greater chance of selecting the correct answer.

As there is no penalty for guessing in the IELTS Test, there is no reason why you shouldn't use the question paper to help you to answer the questions you missed on the tape.

Try the following exercises to help you practise your skill at guessing.

**THERE IS NO TAPE WITH THIS EXERCISE**

*Two students, Malcolm and Sheila, are trying to decide what to do this evening.*

*Circle the correct letter A–D*

1　What is on television at 7.00 p.m.?

　　**A**　a horror film

　　**B**　a program on Russian cooking

　　**C**　the nightly news

　　**D**　the Open University

2　What do they plan to eat?

　　**A**　take-away pizza

　　**B**　the buffet at the Hilton Hotel

　　**C**　roast beef

　　**D**　cornflakes

3　What does Malcolm have to do before tomorrow?

　　**A**　watch a football match on television

　　**B**　telephone his family

　　**C**　telephone his lecturer

　　**D**　pay the telephone bill

**4** Why doesn't Sheila want to go out?

    **A**    she hasn't got any money

    **B**    she's worried about losing her money

    **C**    she needs to borrow some money

    **D**    she has borrowed some money

**5** Why does Malcolm decide to stay up late?

    **A**    to watch a football match on television

    **B**    because he is not tired

    **C**    he has an exam early the next morning

    **D**    because he is going to an all-night party

*Questions 6–10*

*Complete the following news report using* **NO MORE THAN 3 WORDS OR NUMBERS.**

---

**Melcastle Flooded**

Melcastle experienced severe flooding yesterday when the
**(6)** ...................... Mel burst its banks. This follows **(7)** ......................
days of heavy rain. So far 5 people have been reported dead and
another 20 injured. However, many people are still **(8)** ......................
Houses in the affected areas are still under water and often the only
way to travel is by **(9)** ........................ The airport has been shut for
the last three days due to **(10)** ........................................... runways.
An official from the Ministry of Transport said that they hoped to
resume normal services as soon as possible.

---

*Questions 11–12*

*Name* **TWO** *of the problems faced by emergency services.*

*Circle* **TWO** *letters from* **A–E.**

**A**  transportation difficulties

**B**  lack of food

**C**  no electricity

**D**  risk of fire

**E**  lack of money

Now check your answers in the Answer Key on page 94.

# The Listening Test
## Section 2

## What is it?

- It is a monologue; that is, there is only one speaker.
- It is often in two parts.
- You are given time to look at the questions.
- You will not **hear** a spoken example, but there may be a written example in a shaded box in the booklet.
- The topic is one of general interest to any member of the community.

## The Questions

### THE MAIN STRATEGIES ARE

- reading the instructions carefully
- analysing the questions
- predicting possible answers.

### SECTION 2 Questions 12–17

*Questions 12–14*

*Complete the table according to the information given by the police officer.*

| number of cars stolen per year | (12) ............................... |
| number of cars recovered | (13) ............................... |
| number of cars not locked | (14) ............................... |

*Questions 15–17.*

*Write **NO MORE THAN THREE WORDS** for each answer.*

What are the two kinds of car thieves?

15 _____

16 _____

Which kind of car thief is likely to use a stolen car for committing a crime?

**17** _____

## How to Answer—Demonstration

### STEP 1—OVERVIEW OF THE INSTRUCTIONS

The instruction for questions 12–17 tells you to complete a table. It does not give you any information about what to write in the table. You will have to look at the table itself to see what you need to write into it.

Now look at the instruction for questions 15–17. It tells you to answer in **NO MORE THAN THREE WORDS**. This means that the answer might be one word, two words or three words, but it will **not** be four words. You should also know that these answers never require a contraction like *wasn't*.

### STEP 2—READ THE QUESTIONS AND STUDY HOW YOU HAVE TO ANSWER

**What you can expect to hear**

In this test you will hear a police officer giving a talk about ways to prevent motor vehicle theft. By looking at the table for questions 12–14 you can see that the speaker will give some statistics about motor vehicle theft. So you know you will be listening for **numbers**.

**What you have to do**

Sometimes you will not hear numbers in exactly the form of the questions. You might have to make a simple calculation, as you did for question 7 in Section 1. If you use the time given for studying the questions, you will know exactly what kind of information is needed. Then you can quickly put the numbers in as you listen. Also, remember that you can write the numbers as either numerals or words, or even a combination. So it would be easier to write a number like 108 as a numeral, but a number like 5 billion as a combination of a numeral and a word.

In some tests you might have to answer a question with a combination of numerals and letters, as might be used in a car registration number or a student registration number. You will find an example of this type of question in Practice Listening test 2 (page 36). Listening exercise 1 on page 29 will give you practice in listening for numbers, letters and names of places.

Analyse questions 15–17. What can you expect to hear? What do you have to do?

What kind of information are they asking for?

Actually, the first question requires two answers, which is why it has two numbers. The key words in this question are:

What are the two kinds of car thieves?

Can you predict any possible answers?

The key words in question 17 are:

<u>Which kind</u> of car thief is likely to use a stolen car for <u>committing a crime</u>?

The use of 'which' in this question tells you that the answer is most likely to be **ONE** of the answers in questions 15 and 16, but you will have to listen very carefully to know which one.

**NOW START YOUR TAPE**

Listen to the first part of the talk and do questions 12–17. Use the short time given to review the questions.

**STOP YOUR TAPE**

when you hear the instruction to do so.

*Questions 18 and 19*

*Question 18*

*Choose the picture A–D which best shows what the police officer says a vehicle owner **SHOULD DO**.*

A

C

B

D

*Question 19*

*Choose the picture A–D which best shows what the police officer says a vehicle owner **SHOULD NOT DO**.*

A

C

B
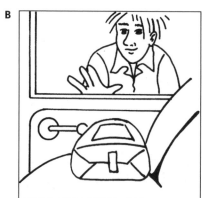

D
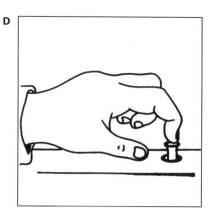

Questions 18 and 19 are based on the second part of the talk about preventing vehicle theft. Look closely at the instructions, the questions and the pictures. Take particular notice of those words in the questions given in **BOLD ITALIC CAPITALS**. These emphasise that the first set of pictures is concerned with what you **SHOULD DO**, or the **right thing to do**, and the second set is concerned with what you **SHOULD NOT DO**, or the **wrong thing to do**.

Although it may not be completely clear what the pictures represent when you first look at them, you will find as you listen to the talk that they all relate quite clearly to what is said. Can you predict what the answers might be? Can you eliminate any of the possibilities? You will now be told to look at the rest of the questions for Section 2 before the final part of the talk.

**START YOUR TAPE**

Use the short time provided to look at questions 18 and 19 again. Listen to the rest of the talk and answer questions 18 and 19.

**STOP YOUR TAPE**

Use the time given at the end to check your answers. Use this time the best way you can by either going over your answers for Section 2 or by reading the questions for Section 3. Continue until you hear the instruction to turn to Section 3.

**STOP YOUR TAPE**

<br>

## T E S T   T I P S

- If you need to write your answers more clearly, do so.

- If you have missed any questions, try to remember the answers.

- If you can't remember an answer, have a guess.

- If you are happy with your answers, go on and study the questions for the next section.

# The Listening Test
# Section 3

## What is it?

- It is a conversation between two or more speakers.
- It is usually in two parts.
- You are given time to look at the questions.
- There is no example on the cassette tape.
- The topic is often related to student life.

## The Questions

### THE MAIN STRATEGIES ARE:

- analysing the questions
- familiarising yourself with the form of the answers
- predicting possible answers
- eliminating unlikely answers
- preparing yourself to distinguish voices.

Now look at the questions for Section 3 of this test.

**SECTION 3   Questions 20–29**

*Questions 20–27*

*Complete the table. Use **NO MORE THAN THREE WORDS** for each answer. (Note: X means information not given.)*

|  | **Reading** | **Essays** | **Lectures** | **Seminars** |
|---|---|---|---|---|
| Lisa | too interesting | handwriting word limit | (23)...................... | (25)...................... |
| Sasha | (20)...................... | (22)...................... | (24)...................... | (26)...................... |
| Olaf | (21)...................... | plagiarism | X | (27)...................... |

*Questions 28 and 29*

*Choose the correct letter A, B, C or D.*

**28** Who are Lisa, Olaf and Sasha?

    **A**    Lisa is a lecturer. Olaf and Sasha are students

    **B**    they are all first year foreign students

    **C**    Olaf and Sasha are foreign students. Lisa is their tutor

    **D**    Lisa is a local student. Olaf and Sasha are foreign students

**29** What does Lisa think of Sasha's last seminar paper?

    **A**    it was like a lecture

    **B**    it was professional

    **C**    it was rather boring

    **D**    she couldn't believe it

## How to Answer—Demonstration

### STEP 1—OVERVIEW OF THE INSTRUCTIONS

You have to complete the tables using **NO MORE THAN THREE WORDS**. Also, look at the note. It tells you that **X** means there is no information given for this box, so you know that you will not hear what problems Olaf has with lectures.

### STEP 2—READ THE QUESTIONS AND STUDY HOW YOU HAVE TO ANSWER

**What you can expect to hear**

The tables show the names of three people and there are four column headings. If there are three people, there must be either two male or two female voices. This means that you will have to distinguish them from each other and work out which voice belongs to which person. You will find an exercise to practise this skill on Cassette 2, Side B.

From the column headings you should already be able to work out that the conversation will probably be about study programs.

For the first part of the conversation, the introduction on the cassette tape tells you that for questions 20–24 the people are talking about study difficulties.

**What you have to do**

Because you know that the people are talking about study *difficulties*, and you can see the headings in the table, you have some clues to possible answers. In other words, you might be able to predict what the answers might be. On the side of the page, note down your ideas about study difficulties people might have in relation to reading, writing essays and listening to lectures. Do not write them in the table at this stage. As you listen you can transfer them to the table, or even just use arrows and write them in during the time you are given at the end of the section.

**NOW START YOUR TAPE**

Listen to the first part of the discussion and answer questions 20–24. When you have finished this section

**STOP YOUR TAPE**

Look back at questions 25–29 on pages 22 and 23.

### What you can expect to hear

For the second part of this section, the instructions on the tape tell you to complete the last column of the table with what they say about seminars. Difficulties are not mentioned. This means that you might hear comments about seminars that include advantages as well as difficulties.

Read questions 28 and 29 carefully and underline the key terms. Note that question 29 asks you for Lisa's *opinion* of Sasha's last seminar paper. Do you expect her to say something good or bad about the paper?

### What you have to do

This time you should make a note of both advantages and difficulties of seminars in the margin of your booklet. It is possible that you can already answer question 28 from the information you have heard so far.

**START YOUR TAPE**

Complete questions 25–29 and then let your tape continue until your hear the instruction to turn to Section 4. Again, use this time either to go over your answers to Section 3 or to go on to look at Section 4.

**STOP YOUR TAPE**

---

### T E S T   T I P S

- Don't worry if you hear a lot of extra information between questions.

- The information you need to answer a question is often repeated.

- The words in the answer choices are often synonyms of the words you hear.

---

# The Listening Test
# Section 4

## *What is it?*

- It is a monologue.
- It is usually not divided into parts, although there may be short pauses.
- There is often a written example in the question booklet, but there is not a separate spoken example.
- The questions to this section are often in the form of notes or a summary to be completed. However, there is sometimes a mixture of question types, as in Listening test Section 3 in this book.
- It is usually a short talk or lecture similar to what you might hear at the beginning of a course, but you do not need specialist knowledge to understand the ideas presented.

## The Questions

### THE MAIN STRATEGIES ARE:

- reading the notes or summary quickly
- predicting possible answers
- taking notes as you listen.

### SECTION 4  *Questions 30–40*

*Complete the following lecture summary. Write **NO MORE THAN THREE WORDS** for each answer.*

| South-East Asian Traditions | |
|---|---|
| *Example* | *Answer* |
| Course Coordinator | Paul Stange |

- **Course materials**

    two textbooks—Osborne and Legge

    *lecture notes*  (30) ............................................................

    *study guide*  (31) ............................................................

    *continued overleaf*

library
bookshop
easier
more diff than

history

countries?
the West

relationships/
connections

base
foundation

can get textbooks from **(32)** ........................... and other materials from Paul Stange after this lecture.

Two of the readings difficult, but Bender **(33)**...................... Smail

Both very important because help develop **(34)** ...........................

- **Course structure**

Main course focus is on **(35)** ........................... of South-East Asia.

Influences from **(36)** ......................... and **(37)** ........................... .

These influences have been both **(38)** ........................... and social.

The emphasis is on **(39)** ........................... between past influences and present cultural patterns.

- **Relation to other courses**

Later courses focus more on political and economic aspects of modern period.   ·

This course serves as **(40)** ..................................... to later courses.

# How to Answer—Demonstration

## STEP 1—OVERVIEW OF THE INSTRUCTIONS

The instructions in this practice material are basically the same as for Section 3, questions 20–27. You have to answer in **NO MORE THAN THREE WORDS**. However this time you are completing a lecture summary, rather than a table.

## STEP 2—READ THE QUESTIONS AND STUDY THE LECTURE SUMMARY

**What you can expect to hear**

The summary notes give you a general idea of what the whole lecture is about. The skill of skim reading is very useful for overviewing summary notes. A quick reading of the notes, paying attention to the way in which the summary is organised will tell you a lot about what you can expect to hear. The subheadings will tell you the main points the lecture covers. For this exercise, you can see that for questions 30 to 34 you are dealing with the course materials, for questions 35 to 39, you will hear about the course structure, and for question 40 you will hear about the relation of this course to other courses.

**What you have to do**

Study the summary and note down your ideas of what the answers might be. We have written a couple of possibilities in the margin for this example. See what you can add to them.

- The first thing to note is the **heading** at the top of the summary. It tells you that the lecture is about traditions in South-East Asia. What kind of traditions might they be? Can you get any clues from the notes?
- Questions 30 and 31. What other *course materials* might you expect to need for such a course?
- Question 32. *Where*, or *from whom*, might you expect to get your textbooks?
- Question 33. The sentence structure gives you a clue that this question probably requires a *comparison* between the two textbooks, so the words might include 'more…than' or 'less…than' or some other form of a comparative. Looking at the rest of the sentence and the one that follows, you suspect that one book is *more difficult* than the other, so think of some other expressions with this meaning that you might expect to hear. If you hear a word that means the same as difficult, for example, you could still write 'more difficult than' or 'less difficult than' as appropriate, and be correct.
- Question 34 asks you what the two textbooks help to develop. What can you develop by reading a textbook?

The second part of this lecture is concerned with the course structure. It looks at the *focus* and *emphasis* of the course and at *influences* in *South-East Asia*. Here it is useful to keep the heading in mind. The introduction on the cassette tells you that the course is an *introduction*. On what aspects of *South-East Asia* would you expect an introductory course to concentrate? You can see from the notes that the other aspect looked at here relates to influences. What kind of influences do you think they might be and who or what did the influencing?

The final question, question 40, asks you about the relation to other courses, and specifically to *later* courses. What kind of relationship does an introductory course usually have to a later course? Study the question page for this section (pp. 25–6), and consider the way in which a test candidate might have marked the sheet before the section began. Add your own notes and underlining to the page.

### NOW START YOUR TAPE

Listen to Section four and complete the summary.

### STOP YOUR TAPE

when it tells you that you have half a minute to check your answers. At the end of the Listening test you are always given time to go back through the whole test and complete any answers you have not filled in yet. It is extremely unlikely that you will be able to recall any detailed information, particularly from the earlier parts of the test. What you can do is write in any answers from notes you may have made in the margin. You can also check carefully that you have marked exactly what the instructions require.

You will then have ten minutes to transfer all your answers to the answer sheet. In a real test the timing for this is incorporated into the test cassette. For the tests in this book, you will have to time yourself. It is important that you transfer your answers appropriately. If you are instructed to circle the letters in the test booklet, make sure you transfer those letters and not the actual answers, so as not to waste time. For questions requiring no more than three words, make sure this is the maximum number of words you write.

Use the time to check all your answers until you hear the final instruction to stop your tape.

Give yourself ten minutes to transfer your answers to the answer sheet. You can check your answers with the Answer Key in the Appendix. You can also find the transcript of this test on page 67.

There are two more Practice tests (Practice test 2 and Practice test 3) at the end of this section. You may photocopy these booklets. The recording for Practice test 2 is on Side B of Cassette 1. The recording for Practice test 3 is on Side A of Cassette 2.

## T E S T   T I P S

- Although questions can be answered in pen or pencil you will need a *soft* pencil to fill in your candidate number and other information.

- Even if you can't answer most of the questions in Section 1, don't panic. Often people who make mistakes early in the test end up getting very good marks.

- If you don't know the answer to a question, guess. There are no points taken off for wrong answers.

- Try and predict the answers before you hear the tape. The test is much easier if you have some idea of what you are listening for before you listen.

- Don't try to listen to every word. Listen specifically for the answers to the questions.

- If you don't hear the answer to a question, go on to the next. It is only one mark lost.

- Make sure you follow the instructions. You may not receive marks for answers written incorrectly onto the answer sheet.

- Often there is a large amount of dialogue between questions. So don't worry if you listen for a long time without hearing anything that helps you answer a question.

# Listening Exercise 1

## Names, numbers and places

The conversations for this exercise are on Cassette 2, Side B.

The purpose of this exercise is to give you practice in listening to numbers, letters and place names and writing them while you are listening. Sometimes you hear a speaker checking if they have heard correctly. This will give you practice in selecting the right number, time, place and so on, when you hear more than one.

*Listen and answer the questions below according to the responses you hear. Write your answers as you hear them the first time.*

**1** Could you spell your last name please?

_____

**2** What's your student number?

_____

**3** Do you have a fax number?

_____

**4** What's the registration number of your car?

_____

**5** When do I have to return these books?

_____

**6** What's the number of the bus?

_____

**7** What time should we be there?

_____

**8** Where are they going?

_____

**9** Could you spell that for me please?

_____

**10** How long before that will be ready?

_____

**11** Do you have your membership number handy?

_____

**12** What's the flight number?

_____

**13** What time does it leave?

_____

**14** Do you know her medical card number?

_____

**15** When are your exams?

_____

**16** Can I have your passport number?

_____

**17** I'll need your account number for that.

_____

**18** What is the number of the part for the washing machine?

_____

**19** How old did you say he was?

_____

**20** What percentage of men would you say actually help
with housework?

_____

Before you check your answers against the transcript (page 74), listen again
to the tape, and check for mistakes.

# Listening Exercise 2

## *Who's speaking?*

The conversations for this exercise are on Cassette 2, Side B, immediately after the recording for Exercise 1. The purpose of this exercise is to give you practice in distinguishing voices from one another and identifying who is speaking.

*Listen to the six short conversations and answer the following questions for each.*

### Conversation 1

Speaker 1 = Bruce          Speaker 2 = Greg

Who played tennis on the weekend?

_____

Who likes watching tennis?

_____

Who likes playing golf?

_____

Who prefers swimming in the ocean to swimming in pools?

_____

### Conversation 2

Speaker 1 = Wendy          Speaker 2 = Barbara

Who lost some money on Saturday night?

_____

Who went to a disco on Saturday night?

_____

Who often goes to the horse races?

_____

Who has given up smoking?

_____

### Conversation 3

Speaker 1 = Carolyn      Speaker 2 = Suzanne

Who says sushi is her favourite food?

_____

Who went swimming on Sunday?

_____

Who likes doing yoga?

_____

### Conversation 4

Speaker 1 = Colin      Speaker 2 = Jeremy

Who ran for 5 or 6 kilometres on Saturday?

_____

Who has a stamp collection?

_____

Who had swordfish for lunch?

_____

Who has a garden?

_____

### Conversation 5

Speaker 1 = David      Speaker 2 = Arthur

Who went mountain biking in the park?

_____

Who stayed home on Saturday?

_____

Who works with people all week?

_____

Who likes to be solitary on weekends?

_____

Who likes socialising on weekends?

_____

**Conversation 6**

Speaker 1 = Alison          Speaker 2 = Kathy

Who is usually very busy taking the children to sports practice on the weekends?

_____

Who is usually very active herself?

_____

Who did very little on Saturday?

_____

Who did very little on Sunday?

_____


You can check your answers in the Answer Key.

   **Note:** There is no transcript for this exercise. If you have any mistakes, you can listen again to the recording.

# Listening Exercise 3

## Study strategies

The conversation for this exercise is on Cassette 2, Side B, immediately after the conversations for Exercise 2. This exercise will give you practice in taking notes while you listen. It also gives you good advice about listening strategies.

*Listen to the conversation between two people preparing for an IELTS Test. Elizabeth gives Ira 8 pieces of advice. Write them down in the table below.*

| Useful Strategies for the Listening Test |
| --- |
|  |

You can check your notes against the transcript (page 75).

# Suggestions For Further Practice

There are a number of English language radio stations which broadcast internationally. Among the best known are: the BBC World Service, the Australian Broadcasting Corporation, and the Voice of America.

These stations provide good listening practice. You might find it particularly useful to listen to:

- **news broadcasts**

  Listen to a specific item and try to identify: the names of the people involved, what happened, the time, the place, and any other significant details.

- **sports programs**

  Listen for: the names of places, contestants and teams, the scores and who scored.

- **the weather report**

**Note:** If you want to check that you have understood correctly you can always check for the same information in the newspaper.

It may also be useful to listen to talk shows, interviews and news magazines in order to practise the skills necessary for listening to a dialogue.

The same sort of exercises can be carried out watching television. Programs such as the BBC world channel, the ABC or CNN are useful for this if you are not in a country with English language television broadcasts.

# IELTS PRACTICE TEST

# LISTENING
# TEST 2

**TIME ALLOWED: 30 minutes**

**NUMBER OF QUESTIONS: 40**

---

### *Instructions*

*You will hear a number of different recordings and you will have to answer questions on what you hear.*

*There will be time for you to read the instructions and questions and you will have a chance to check your work.*

*All the recordings will be played **ONCE** only.*

*The test is in four sections. Write your answers in the Listening question booklet.*

**At the end of the test you will be given ten minutes to transfer your answers to an answer sheet.**

*Now turn to Section 1 on page 2.*

Indonesia Australia Language Foundation

---

# SECTION 1 *Questions 1–11*

*Questions 1–3*

*Complete the form. Write **A NUMBER** for each answer.*

| **Request Form** | |
|---|---|
| *Example:*<br>Name: | *Answer:*<br>**Lester  Mackie** |
| Membership No:<br>Mailing address:<br>Fax No:<br>Phone No: | (1)............................................................<br>17 Westmead Road, Annandale<br>(2)............................................................<br>02 579 6363<br>after 5:00 p.m. (3)....................................... |

*Questions 4–6*

*Circle the correct answer  A–D for each question.*

**4**  Why does the caller need the literature?

    **A**   for a student paper        **C**   for research

    **B**   for a newspaper article        **D**   for general interest

**5**  How long can the caller have the books after the date of posting?

    **A**   3 weeks        **C**   5 weeks

    **B**   6 weeks        **D**   2 weeks

**6**  How will the caller pay the fees?

    **A**   credit card        **C**   money order

    **B**   cheque        **D**   cash

*Questions 7–11*

*Look at the booklist below. Write in the boxes the appropriate letter (**A**, **OL**, or **R**) as explained below:*

| | |
|---|---|
| *available in the library* | **A** |
| *out on loan* | **OL** |
| *request from other library* | **R** |

| **Items Requested** | |
|---|:---:|
| *Example:* | *Answer:* |
| Hallsworth, E. G. (1978) *Land and Water Resources of Australia* | **A** |
| **7**   Government publication (1984) *Land Degradation in Australia* | ☐ |
| **8**   Government publication (1993) *Coastal Zone Inquiry Report* | ☐ |
| **9**   Fisher, D.E. (1980) *Environmental Law* | ☐ |
| **10**  Raiswell, R.W. (1980) *Environmental Chemistry* | ☐ |
| **11**  Burns, M. & Assoc. (1989) *The Environmental Impact of Travel and Tourism* | ☐ |

## SECTION 2  *Questions 12–21*

*Questions 12–16*

*Label the library locations by writing* **ONE, TWO OR THREE LETTERS** *next to the list of places.*

| Example: | Answer: |
|----------|---------|
| law library | **A   B** |

| Floors | | |
|--------|----|------------------------|
| 9 | **A** | |
| 8 | **B** | |
| 7 | **C** | information desk, maps |
| 6 | **D** | |
| 5 | **E** | |
| 4 | **F** | |
| 3 | **G** | |
| 2 | **H** | Library Road entrance |
| 1 | **I** | library lawn entrance |

| | | |
|---|----|---------------------------|
| 4 | **J** | |
| 3 | **K** | |
| 2 | **L** | Mathews building entrance |

**Mathews building annex**

**Main building**

12 loans and returns .....................

13 social sciences and humanities library ....................

14 multimedia and newspapers ....................

15 physical sciences library ...................

16 biomedical library ...................

Complete the notes of general information on the library.

Write **NO MORE THAN THREE WORDS** for each answer.

**General Library Information**

- Eating, drinking and smoking are forbidden in the library.

- Telephones are located on the first floor of the main building.

- Clocks are in the **(17)** ...................................

- There are four **(18)** ......................................

- Toilets are located near the lifts.

- Women's toilets are on **(19)** ................................... floors.

- Men's toilets are on **(20)** ................................ floors.

- Wheelchair access toilets are on floors **(21)** .................................

## SECTION 3  *Questions 22–31*

*Questions 22–23*

Complete the form. Write **NO MORE THAN THREE WORDS OR A NUMBER** for each answer.

<table>
<tr><td colspan="4" align="center">Student Record Card</td></tr>
<tr>
<td>Name:<br>Address:<br>Student number:</td>
<td colspan="3">David Simmons<br>15 Market Ave, Hornsby<br>(22).................................</td>
</tr>
<tr><td colspan="4" align="center">Prerequisites Completed</td></tr>
<tr>
<td></td>
<td>Yes</td>
<td>No</td>
<td>If no—reason</td>
</tr>
<tr>
<td>Screen Studies<br><br>18 credit points</td>
<td><br><br>✓</td>
<td>✓</td>
<td>(23)...................</td>
</tr>
</table>

*Question 24*

Circle the two examination dates.

|     | JUNE |    |    |    |    |     | JULY |    |    |    |
|-----|------|----|----|----|----|-----|------|----|----|----|
| **Sun** | 1 | 8 | 15 | 22 | 29 |     | 6 | 13 | 20 | 27 |
| **Mon** | 2 | 9 | 16 | 23 | 30 |     | 7 | 14 | 21 | 28 |
| **Tue** | 3 | 10 | 17 | 24 |    | 1 | 8 | 15 | 22 | 29 |
| **Wed** | 4 | 11 | 18 | 25 |    | 2 | 9 | 16 | 23 | 30 |
| **Thu** | 5 | 12 | 19 | 26 |    | 3 | 10 | 17 | 24 | 31 |
| **Fri** | 6 | 13 | 20 | 27 |    | 4 | 11 | 18 | 25 |    |
| **Sat** | 7 | 14 | 21 | 28 |    | 5 | 12 | 19 | 26 |    |

*Questions 25–29*

*Circle the correct answer A–D*

**25** Dr Richardson explains that the set exercises

   **A**   require reference to a wide range of resources

   **B**   should be at least 250 words in length

   **C**   focus on key terms and concepts in media studies

   **D**   do not have fixed answers

**26** Dr Richardson explains that essays one and two

   **A**   are to be the same length

   **B**   should both be analytical

   **C**   both emphasise studies of audiences

   **D**   should be especially easy for David

*How does Dr Richardson describe each of the assignments?*

*Complete the table by writing **ONE OR TWO** appropriate letters (**M, T, A or J**) as explained below:*

| | | | |
|---|---|---|---|
| *mechanical* | **M** | *theoretical* | **T** |
| *analytical* | **A** | *journalistic* | **J** |

| Assignment | Description |
|---|---|
| Set exercises | **(27)** ................. |
| Assignment 1 | **(28)** ................. |
| Assignment 2 | **A** |
| Assignment 3 | **(29)** ................. |

*Questions 30–31*

*Circle the correct answer.*

**30** Which two time slots does Dr Richardson suggest David use for his essay?

    **A**   the six o'clock and the mid-morning

    **B**   the breakfast and the six o'clock

    **C**   the mid-morning and the midnight

    **D**   the midday and the ten o'clock

*Write the answer using* **NO MORE THAN THREE WORDS**

**31** What will David do before he decides which part of the programs to use?

.............................................................................................................................

# SECTION 4  *Questions 32–40*

*Questions 32–40*

*Complete the summary. Write* **NO MORE THAN THREE WORDS** *for each answer.*

| **Coastal Zone Inquiry** | |
|---|---|
| *Example* <br> Speaker: | *Answer* <br> Kevin Ackroyd |

**BACKGROUND:**

Problem: pressure on **(32)**.....................................

This pressure caused by **(33)**.....................................

Contributing factors:

- economic development

- **(34)**.....................................

- industrial expansion

- **(35)**.....................................

Two factors that are particularly important:

- **(36)**..................................... likely to continue

- industry, especially tourism which competes with **(37)**..................................... farming industries

**CONCLUSIONS:**

Need to
- raise profile of coastal zone

- exercise greater vision

- **(38)**.....................................

**RECOMMENDATIONS:**

Need for
- long-term view

- broad view

- modern **(39)**.....................................

- consultation with **(40)**.....................................

# IELTS PRACTICE TEST

# LISTENING
## TEST 3

**TIME ALLOWED: 30 minutes**

**NUMBER OF QUESTIONS: 40**

---

### *Instructions*

*You will hear a number of different recordings and you will have to answer questions on what you hear.*

*There will be time for you to read the instructions and questions and you will have a chance to check your work.*

*All the recordings will be played **ONCE** only.*

*The test is in four sections. Write your answers in the Listening question booklet.*

***At the end of the test you will be given ten minutes to transfer your answers to an answer sheet.***

*Now turn to Section 1 on page 2.*

Indonesia Australia Language Foundation

# SECTION 1 *Questions 1–9*

*Questions 1–6*

Complete the table comparing the two towns. Write **NO MORE THAN THREE WORDS** for each answer.

|  | **Albany** | **Watford** |
|---|---|---|
| **Distance from nearest city** | *Example:* **150 miles** | 17 miles |
| **Population** | (1)........................... | 80–90 000 |
| **Advantages** | friendly, relaxed slow pace of life | good entertainment |
| **Disadvantages** | (2)........................... no jobs | (4)........................... crime |
| **Main industry** | (3)........................... | electronics light engineering |
| **Climate** | wet and windy | (5)........................... |
| **Main attractions** | beautiful beaches | (6)........................... |

*Questions 7–9*

*Write **NO MORE THAN THREE WORDS** for each answer.*

7  What does Gordon like about where he is living now?

   ...................................................................

8  When does Maureen think she might go back to Albany?

   ...................................................................

9  How long is Gordon's new contract?

   ...................................................................

# SECTION 2  *Questions 10–19*

*Questions 10–12*

*Listen to the directions and match the places in questions 10–12 to the appropriate letters **A–G** on the map.*

| *Example:* | main stage | *Answer* | .....**A**..... |
| --- | --- | --- | --- |

**10** first aid post          .................

**11** public telephones      .................

**12** security post          .................

C

E

D

A

B

STAGE 3

STAGE 2

F

MAIN ENTRANCE

G

CAR
PARK

N

*Questions 13–14*

*Complete the notes below. Write **NO MORE THAN THREE WORDS** for each answer.*

**13** If you want to be readmitted to the stadium, you must ...................................................

**14** There won't be a festival next year, if there are        ...................................................

*Questions 15–19*

*Complete the table with information about the festival program. Write **NO MORE THAN THREE WORDS OR NUMBERS** for each answer.*

| Name | Type of act | Stage | Time |
|---|---|---|---|
| Brazilian Drum Band | drum band | *Example:* .......**3**....... | 7.00 |
| Claude and Jacques | mime artists | 3 | 8.00 |
| Great Grapefruit | **(15)**................ | 2 | 7.00 |
| Crossed Wires | jazz fusion | 1 | **(16)**................ |
| Tom Cobble | comedian | 1 | 10.30 |
| Flying Barito Brothers | acrobats | **(17)**................ | 9.00 |
| Winston Smiles | reggae singer | 3 | **(18)**................ |
| Great Mysteron | magic and illusion | 2 | 9.30 |
| Blue Grass Ben | **(19)**................ | 2 | 12.00 |
| The Proffets | music group | 1 | 12.00 |

# SECTION 3   *Questions 20–29*

*Questions 20–21*

*Circle the correct answer A–D*

**20** What does Frank have to do next?

    **A**   get the results of the survey back

    **B**   draw the results of the survey

    **C**   make some conclusions

    **D**   collect more information

**21** What is Theresa's market research project on?

    **A**   violence on television

    **B**   transportation in the city

    **C**   the history of transportation

    **D**   bureaucracy in the city

**22** What did the results of Frank's survey show?

    **A**   everyone thinks there is too much violence on TV

    **B**   most people think there is too much violence on TV

    **C**   there is no real agreement on the amount of violence

    **D**   there is a problem with the survey

*Questions 23–25*

*Complete the summary. Write* **NO MORE THAN THREE WORDS** *for each answer.*

---

**Summary**

Children might see the heroes of violent films as **(23)**.........................................................

so most people think that violent programs should only be shown after 10.00p.m.

However, there is a **(24)**......................................... who feel that violent films

should be banned. Although news broadcasts are violent, people felt they shouldn't be

banned as they are **(25)**...........................................

---

*Questions 26–29*

*Write the answer using* **NO MORE THAN THREE WORDS OR NUMBERS**.

**26** How many questionnaires did Frank get back? .................................................................

**27** Theresa says Frank's survey doesn't represent ................................................................

**28** Where is Theresa going to interview her respondents? ....................................................

**29** The best type of questions are ....................................................................................

# SECTION 4   *Questions 30–40*

*Questions 30–35*

*Complete the notes. Write **NO MORE THAN ONE NUMBER OR THREE WORDS** for each answer.*

| Quality Control |
|---|
| *Example:*<br>Quality control is more than an inspection of **the finished product** |

*Finished product inspection*

The main disadvantage of finished product inspection is that it cannot make

(30)....................................................

*Quality control as a continuous process*

Manufacturers usually consider quality control to be an ongoing process.

The advantages are:   (31) ..........................................................

(32) ..........................................................

It is easier to detect faults on components.

*Raw material inspection*

There is no point in processing defective raw materials.

Eighty-seven per cent of large firms and (33).......................................................... of small firms have a standard raw material inspection procedure.

It is also useful to inspect incoming components.

*What are we testing for?*

Although the testing for an expensive car and a child's toy is very different in both cases the main priority is (34) ..........................................................

Function testing answers the question: Does the product do what it's supposed to?

*Formal defects investigation*

Usually used by high-tech industries.

*Environmental impact report*

Testing must assess the impact of both the product itself and

(35) ..........................................................

*Questions 36–37*

*Circle the correct letter **A–C** for each question.*

**36** .......... of companies have standards in line with the Standards Association of Australia.

  **A**  87%

  **B**  80%

  **C**  65%

**37** .......... of companies have quality control regulations which apply international standards.

  **A**  22%

  **B**  23%

  **C**  65%

**38** Which of the following pie charts best represents the level of the people responsible for quality control?

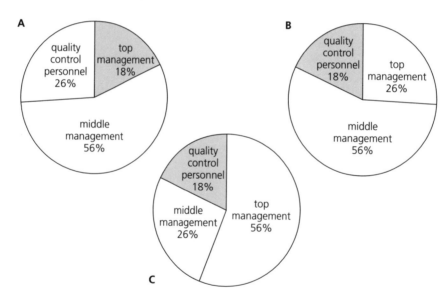

*Questions 39–40*

*Name **TWO** of the effects of releasing low quality products*

*Circle **TWO** letters **A–E**.*

**A**  danger of lawsuits           **B**  loss of customer goodwill

**C**  wasted production time       **D**  compensation costs

**E**  bankruptcy

# The Speaking Test

# What To Expect

Basically the IELTS Speaking test is a 10–15 minute interview or conversation between a candidate and an examiner. The Speaking test is the final section of the IELTS Test.

At the end of the Writing section of the test you will be given a form to fill in. This form requires some basic information about you, your career, your study plans and your hobbies. The aim of this form is to give the examiner some information to provide topics to ask about in the interview. You will find an example of the form on page 98.

The interviewer is a certified examiner appointed by the test centre and approved by UCLES.

**Note:** All interviews are recorded so that UCLES can check that the correct interview procedure is followed and that an accurate band score is given.

According to the official handbook the Speaking test has five phases which are described in the following table.

---

1  **Introduction**
   The examiner and candidate introduce themselves. The candidate is made to feel comfortable and encouraged to talk briefly about his or her life, home, work and interests.
2  **Extended discourse**
   The candidate is encouraged to speak at length about some familiar topic, which is either of general interest or of relevance to his or her culture, place of living, or country of origin. This stage involves explanation, description or narration.

---

3 **Elicitation**
  The candidate is given a task card with some information on it and is encouraged to take the initiative by asking questions either to elicit information or to solve a problem. Tasks are based on 'information gap' type activities.
4 **Speculation and attitudes**
  The candidate is encouraged to talk about future plans and the proposed course of study. Alternatively, the examiner may choose to return to a topic raised earlier.
5 **Conclusion**
  The interview is concluded.

# Phase 1—Introduction

Phase 1 of the IELTS Test is the introduction. You should:
- state clearly your name and candidate number into the microphone for identification purposes
- ask what you should call the examiner if he or she doesn't tell you.

# Phase 2—About Yourself

During this stage of the test, the examiner will try to find out as much as possible about you as a person.

### R E M E M B E R

The more information you give at this point, the easier it will be for the examiner to hold a conversation, and the more impressed he or she will be with your fluency. Therefore, don't give one word answers such as 'yes' or 'no'.

## *Practice*

This section is designed to give you a chance to think about the type of questions you might get asked in Stage 2 of the Speaking test. All the topics included in these exercises are likely to be used for questions in this phase of the test.

**Personal information**
  The following line represents your life from your birth to now. Put the ten most important events in your life on the line.

birth                                                              now

Think of two questions an examiner might ask about each event, and write the questions in the space provided.

```



```

## Family and hobbies

Often an examiner will ask you about your family and hobbies as a way of getting to know you. Fill in the following tables so it is easier to answer this type of question.

| Family member | Age | Job / School | Point of Interest |
|---|---|---|---|
| *Example: brother* | | | |

| Things I like to do | Things I hate to do |
|---|---|
| 1 | 1 |
| 2 | 2 |
| 3 | 3 |
| 4 | 4 |
| 5 | 5 |

Next, try to think of questions that need longer answers, giving information for each of the activities in your table. If, for example, you write 'I like travelling', possible questions could be as follows.

**Where** is the most interesting place you have been?

**Where** would you most like to go?

**How** did you travel there?

**When** did you go there?

**Why** do you like travelling?

With **whom** do you usually go?

**What** do you think is the most important thing to take with you, apart from your passport and money?

**Which** country would you most like to live in?

When you have decided on questions for your likes and dislikes, provide possible answers.

**Your job**

Think about the following topics:

- the form of transport used to go to work
- your daily routine and responsibilities
- the aspects of your job that you like
- what you dislike about your job.

Try to predict the type of conversation you might have with an examiner on this subject.

**Your school**

Think about the following topics:

- how you get to school
- the size of your school, the number of pupils
- the subjects you like and dislike
- education in your country compared to the country where you plan to go.

Anticipate the type of conversation you might have with an examiner on this subject.

**Your home town**

You are an information officer at your local tourist bureau. Prepare a short guide giving places of interest, customs and useful advice for visitors to the area.

# Phase 3—Asking Questions

In the elicitation section the examiner will give you a task card. You have to ask questions based on the card's information to find out about the situation from the examiner, who is playing a role.

The task card the examiner gives you looks something like this.

---

**Sample Task 1**      **Booking a Holiday**

**The examiner has just booked a holiday at the travel agent. Find out some information about the holiday.**

Find out about:
- the destination
- the form of transport
- the length of the holiday
- the dates of the holiday
- the number of people going
- the reason for the holiday

---

You will have some time to read your task card and then you should begin asking questions.

### R E M E M B E R

- you can ask questions other than the ones indicated on the card

- the examiner is playing a role and you should stick to the topic on the card

- you are being assessed and not the examiner, so you should do most of the talking.

## *Practice*

Look at the sample role card and try to think of as many questions to ask as possible. It may help to think of all the 'Wh' words (including how) and make them into questions relevant to the topic. Then, complete the following interview task.

## INTERVIEW TASK

*Fill in the candidate's questions in the conversation below.*

**C** = Candidate

**E** = Examiner

**C** _____?

**E** I'm going to Spain.

**C** _____?

**E** We're catching the train to Madrid.

**C** _____?

**E** We'll stay there for 2 or 3 days.

**C** _____?

**E** After that we're going to the Costa Del Sol.

**C** _____?

**E** Oh, about 3 weeks altogether.

**C** _____?

**E** Next Saturday.

**C** _____?

**E** Some friends from my course.

**C** _____?

**E** To celebrate the end of our course.


## LATERAL THINKING

Work with a partner. Ask your partner Yes/No questions to find out the solution to the problems below.

1   Romeo and Juliet lie dead on the floor of an apartment. By their side is some water, some broken glass and a cat. What happened?

2   A man is pushing a car towards a hotel. If the car stops at the hotel he will be bankrupt. Why?

3   A man lives on the 25th floor of an apartment block. Every morning, he catches the lift down to the ground floor. Every evening he catches the lift up to the 15th floor and then walks up the last 10 floors. Why?

**4** There is a dead man on the side of a mountain with half a match in his hand. What happened?

**5** A man is standing in the corner of a room with a bag of tools by his side. After 2 hours the man smiles, picks up his tools and walks out. Why?

## AN ADVERTISEMENT

The information to complete this table is on page 65. Ask a partner questions to find out the missing information. Write down your partner's information in the gaps.

---

**House for rent**

In the ............................... close to the

...............................

Includes:

...... bedrooms

...... bathrooms

large living room

A$ ............... a week

contact: ...............................

telephone:  ...........................

---

## PRACTICE TASK 2

---

**Sample Task 2       Renting a Car**

**You are interested in renting a car for a few days. Your examiner is in charge of a car rental agency.**

**Find out some information about renting cars.**

Find out about:
- the cost per day
- the cost per kilometre
- insurance
- the type of driving licence required
- the type of car available
- the pick-up point for the car

---

**Note:** there is an interviewer's card on page 66.

> **Sample Task 3     Repairing your Computer**
>
> **Your computer is broken. Your examiner works in a computer shop. He/she has looked at the computer and is ready to tell you about the problem.**
>
> Find out about:
> - the problem
> - the possible cause of the problem
> - the time needed for repairs
> - parts that need to be ordered
> - the cost of repairs
> - the guarantee

**Note:** there is an interviewer's card on page 66.

# Phase 4—Wider Issues

In this section of the test the interviewer will ask you to give more in-depth answers. Often you will be asked to share your future plans or to talk in greater detail about a topic introduced in Section 2 of the Speaking test.

Possible topics include:
- Poverty and wealth
- Pollution
- Globalisation
- Development

## Practice

**'Before I die I want to ...'**

In the following space think of as many things that you want to do in the future as possible. Try to put a time scale on your plans using the timeline below.

```
|                                                              |
now                                              distant future
```

## STUDYING ABROAD

List the reasons why you have chosen to study abroad.

| Reasons for studying abroad |
| --- |
| |

## PROBLEMS

Think of problems that you might encounter while studying overseas and ways of overcoming them. Complete the table below.

| Problems that might be expected | Ways of dealing with these problems |
| --- | --- |
| | |

## THE FUTURE

Imagine it is the year 2020. How do you think the world will have changed? Jot down some ideas in the following table. Use these topics to help you.

- Technology
- Lifestyle
- Economics
- Your country
- The environment
- Problems the world will face

## YOUR JOB

Describe the job you would like in the future in the space provided.

To do this job, what type of person do you need to be?

*For example:* To be a doctor you have to have a degree in medicine so you must be prepared to study very hard. A doctor has to work long hours so you must be physically fit. You must be able to get on with people so that your patients trust you and you mustn't be scared of blood.

## SPEAKING TIPS—TRUE OR FALSE?

Look at the following statements about the IELTS Speaking test and decide if they are true or false.

1 The IELTS Speaking test is basically a grammar test.
2 It is not a good idea to memorise answers.
3 You shouldn't say anything, if you think you might make a mistake.
4 You should know exactly what you are going to say before you go into the test.
5 You should try to give as much information about yourself as possible.
6 The interviewer always asks the same questions.
7 A panel of assessors will listen to the tape of your interview after the test.
8 You shouldn't ask the examiner personal questions.

9 You are assessed on an overall impression of your language speaking ability.

10 The interview is the easiest section of the test.

You will find answers to this exercise in the Appendix on page 96.

# Practice Interviews

On Cassette 2, Side B you will hear questions from two practice interviews. Answer the questions as if you were doing a real IELTS interview. Stop the tape when you hear the beeps to give yourself time to answer the questions.

The following situation cards are for Phase 3 of the Practice test. When you reach this phase in each of the interviews, stop the tape and give yourself a few minutes to study the card.

## Practice Interview 1

**Sample Task 3       An Accident**

**The examiner has just seen an accident. Find out some information about what happened.**

Find out about:
- the time of accident
- what the examiner was doing
- the accident itself
- where the accident took place
- the number of people injured
- the cause of the accident

## Practice Interview 2

**Sample Task 4       Visitors**

**The interviewer has visitors from overseas. Find out some information about them.**

Find out :
- who they are
- where they are from
- how they became friends
- the length of their stay
- their plans for daytime and evening activities

**Lateral thinking answers**

**1**  Romeo and Juliet are goldfish. The cat knocked over the goldfish bowl.

**2**  They are playing monopoly.

**3**  The man is too short to press the 25th floor button.

**4**  The man was a passenger on a plane flying over the mountains. The plane was too heavy so the passengers had to draw lots to see who had to jump. The dead man chose the half match and had to jump from the airplane.

**5**  The man painted the floor and forgot to leave himself a way out of the room. Therefore he must wait 2 hours for the paint to dry before leaving.

**An advertisement**

---

**House for rent**

In the Kings Cross area close to the railway station.

Includes:

4 bedrooms

2 bathrooms

large living room

A$200.00 a week

contact Mr Kapinski

telephone: 01 935 7619

---

Practice Task 2—Interviewer's card

---

**Sample Task 2        Renting a Car**

**You are interested in renting a car for a few days. Your examiner is in charge of a car rental agency.**

**Find out some information about renting cars.**

Find out about:
- the cost per day
- the cost per kilometre
- insurance
- the type of driving licence required
- the type of car available
- the pick-up point for the car

---

The information below will help you answer your partner's questions:
- A$ 20.00 per day
- A$ 0.50 per kilometre—first 100 kilometres free
- comprehensive insurance is included in the price of the car
- drivers need an Australian or an international licence
- Honda Civic or Toyota Starlet
- the agency will deliver.

Practice Task 3—Interviewer's card

---

**Sample Task 3        Repairing your Computer**

**Your computer is broken. Your examiner works in a computer shop. He has looked at the computer and is ready to tell you about the problem.**

Find out about:
- the problem
- the possible cause of the problem
- the time needed for repairs
- parts that need to be ordered
- the cost of repairs
- the guarantee

---

Use the following information to answer your partner's questions:
- the computer has a virus
- the virus was probably caught from an infected disk
- about 2 days
- a new disk drive
- A$100.00
- 6 months.

# Listening Transcripts

## Practice Listening Test 1

*You will hear a number of different recordings and you will have to answer questions on what you hear. There will be time for you to read the instructions and questions and you will have a chance to check your work. All the recordings will be played **once** only. The test is in four sections. Write all your answers in the Listening question booklet. At the end of the test, you will be given ten minutes to transfer your answers to an answer sheet. Now turn to page 7 of this book.*

**STOP YOUR TAPE**

*You will see that there is an example which has been done for you.*
*On this occasion only the conversation relating to this will be played first.*

| | |
|---|---|
| **Jane** | Hello Steve. How are you? |
| **Steve** | Oh I'm not too bad today, thank you Jane. And you? How did you go in the exams? |
| **Jane** | I'm not sure. I haven't got all my results yet, but I'm so glad we're coming up to the end of the semester. I really need a holiday, so I'm going camping with some friends. |

*Jane is pleased about it being the end of semester, so you choose **C** 'the semester ending'.*

**STOP YOUR TAPE**

*Section 1. You will hear two friends talking about a holiday trip they plan to make.*
*First, look at questions 1 to 7*

**20 seconds**

*At this point you would normally hear the example. Because you have already heard the example it is not repeated here. Now we shall begin. You should answer the questions as you listen because you will not hear the recording a second time. First, you have another chance to look at questions 1 to 7.*

**10 seconds**

*Now listen carefully and answer questions 1 to 7.*

**STOP YOUR TAPE**

| | |
|---|---|
| **Jane** | Hello Steve. How are you? |
| **Steve** | Oh I'm not too bad today, thank you Jane. How are you? How did you go in the exams? |
| **Jane** | I'm not sure. I haven't got all my results yet, but I'm so glad we're coming up to the end of the semester. I really need a holiday, so I'm going camping with some friends. What are you doing over the semester break, Steve? |
| **Steve** | I haven't got any plans yet. I don't really have enough money to fly home. I suppose I could get a part-time job and earn some money, but I don't really want to. Then again, maybe I could start studying for next semester. |
| **Jane** | Mmm. I thought about doing some summer courses, but I decided that's not a good idea. I need a break or I'll get stale. I need to do |

something completely different. You do too. Why don't you join me and my friends on the camping trip?

**Steve**    Well, I don't know really. Would your friends mind?

**Jane**    No, of course not. They'd be happy to have you along. We're going down to the Royal National Park. Have you been there yet?

**Steve**    No, I haven't. It's somewhere south of Sydney isn't it?

**Jane**    Yes, it's about 30 kilometres south of Sydney. We'll be getting an early train from Central to Sutherland. It leaves Central at seven and goes to Waterfall via Sutherland. Amin and Lucy are joining us there because they live in Caringbah.

**Steve**    Oh, I see. That is very early. And who did you say will join the train at Caringbah?

**Jane**    No, not at Caringbah. At Sutherland. Amin and Lucy. Then, from Waterfall, we'll hike to where we're going to be spending the first few days. That's at Garie beach.

**Steve**    What's the park like? Is it on the coast, or inland?

**Jane**    It's on the coast, but it's very big, over 15 000 hectares and there are a couple of rivers, especially one big one, the Hacking.

**Steve**    Can you do anything on this river? Can we go on it?

**Jane**    Oh yeah, lots. You can hire boats—go boating—row boats.

**Steve**    Row boats. Hey, that sounds fun! Um, and what about scuba diving or horse riding? Can we do any of those things?

**Jane**    Well there isn't much point in scuba diving around there as there aren't any reefs or anything, so there's not much underwater life. And because it's a national park, domestic animals aren't allowed.

**Steve**    So what equipment do we need to bring with us if we're going? Do we have to carry all our food for a week?

**Jane**    No. We've organised for the food to go down with a van, so we don't have to carry too much. You know Dave's van. It's a camper with a fridge and cooking things, so we needn't bother with that. But you'll need to bring a sleeping bag. I've got an extra one I can lend you if you haven't got one.

**Steve**    And what type of clothes should I bring? Like, what's the weather going to be like?

**Jane**    Bathers. Definitely bathers 'cause there are beaches, and the river. You can swim in the river. There's some beautiful little swimming holes with waterfalls in the river. Um … good hiking boots, strong boots and socks. I think you need a few pairs of socks because if they get wet it's often difficult to dry them. Otherwise, whatever you prefer to hike in. If you like shorts that's OK.

**Steve**    And what about my bicycle? Should I bring that?

**Jane**    Not really. Well, you could. There are places to cycle, but none of us are cycling this time. But you will need a warm sweater or jacket for the evenings.

**Steve**    So that's a bit of a pity. I rather like cycling, but not really on my own. And do we have to book anything? Like the train, maybe?

**Jane**    No, we don't need to book the train. And we've already booked beds in the youth hostel. We've booked eight beds and so far we've only got six people, so it's fine for you to come along.

**Steve**    And do we need a guide?

*Jane goes on to talk about some of the activities that they can do in the park.*

*Look at questions 8 to 11, the plan of the park and the list of activities.*

**20 seconds**

*As you listen write the appropriate activities in the correct area of the park. Jane does not mention every area of the park. You will have to leave some areas empty and you will not use all of the activities.*

*You will be given time at the end of the conversation to copy your answers against questions 8 to 11.*

**Steve** And do we need a guide?

**Jane** Oh no. Look here's a map. I'll show you. Now, you see these arrows? They're the marked walking trails. This is Waterfall, where we get off the train. Then we'll walk to Garie beach and stay at the hostel there. You see this area beyond the youth hostel, to the south? Those are rocky bluffs and there are lots of animals and birds in this area. You can spend hours just watching them. Now this area here, around Garie itself, has fabulous beaches for swimming and walking, and in some parts there are rock pools with fascinating sea creatures in them.

**Steve** So there are plenty of places to swim.

**Jane** Yeah, there are great places to swim. Then to the north of Garie, along the coast there are some wonderful cliffs to walk along, where you can get spectacular views. We plan to walk along here to this great picnic and barbecue place with a waterfall, called Wattamolla. Lots of people go there just for the day to have a picnic lunch. Of course Dave will have to drive the van.

This area here is Audley.

**Steve** Where? Oh yeah.

**Jane** It's not a town, it's just a place where two rivers join where you can hire rowboats. We'll spend the last day here and then we'll all pile into the van so Dave can drive us back to Sutherland to get the train home.

*Copy the letter for the area of the map and the activity against numbers 8 to 11 in any order.*

**20 seconds**

*That is the end of Section 1. You now have half a minute to check your answers.*

**30 seconds**

*Now turn to Section 2 on page 17 of your book.*

*Section 2. You will hear a member of the local police force giving a talk on prevention of car theft.*

*Look at questions 12 to 19.*

**30 seconds**

*As you listen to the first part of the talk answer questions 12 to 17 according to the information given in the talk.*

Good evening. I know many of you students are the proud owners of your first motor vehicle and this evening I want to talk to you about some of the things you can do to make sure your car or motorbike isn't stolen. I'll start with a few facts and figures to put you in the picture. Car theft is a widespread problem. In this country alone one car is stolen every 32 seconds. That's almost a million cars each year. And of those, 40 per cent are never recovered. And don't think that just because your car might be a bit old and beaten-up looking no one will steal it. Any car can be stolen. Anywhere.

Most thefts occur in residential areas, often from the front of the house or even from inside the garage. Some areas that are especially dangerous are shopping centres and parking lots, particularly at sports events.

Most car thieves don't need to break into the car. They usually gain entry through unlocked doors and many times they find the key in the ignition. In fact, one in five stolen cars had the keys left in the car. Isn't that amazing? Twenty per cent of drivers left the keys in the ignition of an unlocked car!

Who steals cars? Well, there are basically two kinds of car or bike thieves: joyriders aged about 15 to 21, and professionals. This last group usually needs less than one minute to break into a locked car and they often steal cars to use in other crimes such as robberies. You are much less likely to get your car back if it's stolen by a professional, and if it's stolen by a joyrider chances are it'll be a wreck when you do get it back. Joyriders have a very high accident rate.

**STOP YOUR TAPE**

*Before the final part of the talk, look at questions 18 and 19.*

**10 seconds**

*Now you will hear the rest of the talk. Answer questions 18 and 19.*

What can you do to make sure your car isn't stolen? Well, first and most obviously, lock the car when you leave it. That includes locking the boot or hatchback and making sure all the windows are closed. Even a tiny gap allows a thief to insert a wire to prise open the lock button. Of course, don't leave the keys hanging in the ignition. And don't conceal a spare key inside or outside the car—thieves know all the hiding places. If your car breaks down, lock up before you go for help. Even if you can't start the car, a thief may be able to.

Now since dusk to mid-evening are the peak hours for car theft, make sure you park in a well-lit area, preferably where there are plenty of passers-by, say near a busy store or a restaurant. Avoid leaving your keys with a garage or parking-lot attendant: choose the place you park yourself.

Keep your driver's licence and registration in your wallet or purse, not in the glove compartment of your car. You should also have a record of your car's vital statistics both in your wallet and somewhere at home. This can help with recovery in case of theft.

And finally, it's a good idea to install some kind of safety device. There is a range available—from alarm systems that set off a buzzer or siren if an attempt is made to tamper with the car in any way, to fuel shut-off systems and time-delay ignition systems. Displaying a warning sticker will also help deter would-be thieves. They don't want to waste time on trying to steal a protected car.

So, help us put car thieves out of business by using common sense, always locking your car, installing anti-theft devices and cooperating with the police by reporting any attempt at theft.

*That is the end of Section 2. You now have half a minute to check your answers.*
**30 seconds**
*Now turn to Section 3 on page 22 of your book.*

**STOP YOUR TAPE**

*Section 3. In this section you will hear three people discussing university life.*

*Listen to the discussion about reading assignments, essays and lectures. Complete the table by writing in the difficulties they have with reading, writing essays and listening to lectures against questions 20 to 24. Write no more than three words for each answer. First look at questions 20 to 24.*

**30 seconds**
*Now as you listen to the first part of the discussion, answer questions 20 to 24.*

**Lisa**    Oh hello Olaf. I haven't seen you for ages. How are things going?

**Olaf**    Hello Lisa. Hi Sasha. Well it's great studying here, but some things take quite a bit of getting used to. It's not like studying in my country.

**Sasha**    Oh I know. In my country we used to go to lectures and get the lecturer's notes and then we'd use those to write our essays. Here we have to read *so much*. I just can't keep up with it all. How do you find the reading Lisa?

**Lisa**    Yes, I agree there *is* a lot to read, but I don't mind that. In fact, I like the reading. My problem is that it's all so interesting I want to read more and there just isn't the time. And that creates a problem with the essays for me. I feel like I can't cover the topics in the number of words assigned. Look at this assignment for example. I'm supposed to discuss rational choice models for my economics essay in 3000 words. I could write a book on that topic; in fact, several people have. How am I supposed to cover it in 3000 words? Why do they have to impose a word limit anyhow?

**Olaf**    Well Lisa, remember it's just an undergraduate essay. You're only supposed to demonstrate that you understand the concept, not apply it or anything. But I know what Sasha means about having too much to read. I think the most difficult thing with the reading for me though isn't the quantity but all the new words. Words like 'hegemony' and 'teleology', that you need to understand thoroughly. I'm always being told by my tutors that I'm using them wrongly in my essays. And when I try to use them the same way as in the reading, the tutors say it's plagiarism.

**Sasha**    I have a problem like that too. You know, you listen to the lectures and read the books and articles and then you're supposed to come up with your own ideas for the essays. You're so full of everyone else's ideas, where are you going to get your own from? And there's so much to say it's difficult to organise. I spend hours planning an essay and by the time I get to actually writing it all down the deadline is up. I'm always having to ask for an extension. What about you Lisa? You usually get good marks for your essays.

**Lisa**    Yes, that's true. But I'm always doing the final draft in a hurry and then the tutors complain that they can't read my handwriting. I think I'll have to learn to type, but *when*? And that's another thing I never seem to manage enough time for—lectures. Why are there so many, and they're always so early in the morning! I can't ever get out of bed in time for a nine o'clock lecture.

**Olaf**    Well isn't that because you go to so many parties Lisa? If you don't get home till one or two in the morning, how can you ever expect to be awake for a lecture?

**Sasha**    If you ask me, that wouldn't make any difference. Most of the lecturers are so boring they'd put you to sleep anyhow. Why can't they make the lectures more interesting? After all, a lot of the subjects are fascinating, but the lecturers make them sound boring.

**STOP YOUR TAPE**

*Now listen as they discuss seminars and complete the rest of the table by writing in what they say about seminars against questions 25 to 27. Write no more than three words for each answer. Also answer questions 28 and 29. Look at questions 25 to 29.*

**30 seconds**

*Now as you listen answer questions 25 to 29.*

**Lisa**    At least you can't say that about seminars. They're really interesting and I think I get most benefit from them. You always find other students have read different books and articles and so you get lots of new information in a seminar.

**Olaf**    Yes that's true Lisa. But I still don't enjoy them because people disagree with each other all the time, and I don't like that. I don't like to hear people arguing. It really bothers me.

**Sasha**    Oh Olaf, you're supposed to argue in a seminar. And I really appreciate the chance to do that. Where I come from, women aren't supposed to argue or answer back. I do have to admit, however, that I get *very* nervous about having to give presentations. You know, when you have to read a paper. That's really scary!

**Lisa**    Oh Sasha, I can't believe that! That last paper you gave was so professional. In fact I think you could do a better job than the lecturers...

*That is the end of Section 3. You will now have half a minute to check your answers.*

**30 seconds**

*Look at Section 4 on page 25 of your book.*

**STOP YOUR TAPE**

*Section 4. In this section you will hear an introductory lecture to a course on South-East Asia.*

*First read the summary of the lecture made by a student and look at questions 30 to 40.*

**30 seconds**

*As you listen complete the summary, using no more than three words for each answer. The first one has been done for you as an example.*

My name is Paul Stange. I'm the coordinator of this course. It's called South-East Asian Traditions. I'm also the author of the study guide and course reader and you should have those in front of you. As well as these you'll need two textbooks for the course; there's the one by Osborne and there's another by Legge. I'll talk a bit more about the reading materials in a moment. Now if you haven't got these materials, you can buy the textbooks at the university book shop and you can collect the study guide and the course reader from me on your way out of the lecture.

*[pause of 5 seconds]*

The purpose of this lecture is simply orientation. What I'm going to do is introduce myself, talk you through the course, and give you some additional advice—apart from what's contained in the study guide—on dealing with the various assignments for the course.

First of all, the materials. You'll find the two textbooks very clear and they give a good, basic coverage of the history of the region. Most of the readings in the reader are fairly easy going, but I have to warn you that two of them are quite difficult. These are the readings by Smail and Bender. And, of these two, the one by Bender is perhaps the more challenging. But don't let that put you off, because understanding these two readings is important to help you develop a clearer understanding of the cultures. In other words they'll help you acquire greater sensitivity to the differences between the various cultures in the region.

*[pause of 5 seconds]*

Now, the course itself. The course has multiple aims. It's primarily a history course, but it's not only a history course. It is, in most respects, a cultural history course focusing on South-East Asia. Nevertheless the course is, as you'll see from the materials, an introduction to the South-East Asian studies components of the Asian studies program.

In looking at the cultural history of South-East Asia there are two major influences to be considered: the Chinese and the Indian. It is important not to forget the extensive influence that these two countries have had in the region. China has been trading throughout the region since at least the sixth century, so many of its cultural and social traditions have influenced the countries in the area. And religious practices from India have helped form today's culture. So we'll be looking for the links and the connections between traditional patterns and today's developments in the region.

I think you can now begin to see how these past influences might form a background for the present-day social practices. And in the same way this course will form a basis or background for second and third year courses, with their focus on the modern period, and in particular the economic and political situation of the region.

So that's the outline of the course. I'd like to go on now to look at what *you* have to do, your assignments and so on.

*That is the end of the Listening test. You now have half a minute to check your answers.*
**30 seconds**

***STOP YOUR TAPE***

*[pause] You now have ten minutes to transfer your answers to the Listening answer sheet.*

***STOP YOUR TAPE***

*Listen to these short conversations and use the information you hear to answer the questions in your book. Study the questions first, and try to write the answer while you are listening.*

1   Could you spell your last name please?
    *Yes, certainly. It's G-R-E-A-V-E-S.*

2   What's your student number?
    *J 3 0 4 W-M-B.*

3   Do you have a fax number?
    *It's 02 173 926.*

4   And what's the registration number of your car?
    *B-V 9 2 5 8 J-G.*

5   When do I have to return these books?
    *By 15 July.*

6   What's the number of the bus?
    *Seventy.*
    The number 17?
    *Seventy.*

7   What time should we be there?
    *Not too early. About 9:00.*

8   Where are they going?
    *To Budapest.*
    Was that Bucharest?
    *No, Budapest.*

9   Could you spell that for me please?
    *V-E-X-A-T-I-O-U-S.*

10   How long before that will be ready?
    *It usually takes a couple of weeks, so I'd say the 30th.*

11   Do you have your membership number handy?
    *Yeah. J 2 3 I-A.*

12   What's the flight number?
    *QF 518.*

13   What time does it leave?
    *14:00 hours.*

14   Do you know her medical card number?
    *P-N 9 6 K-J.*

15   When are your exams?
    *On the 16th and the 19th.*

16   Can I have your passport number?
    *9 1 2 00 8 C-Y.*

17   I'll need your account number for that.
    *Fine. It's 300674–4115–18.*

18   Can I help you madam?
    *I need a new spindle for a washing machine.*
    Do you know the part number?
    *Yeah, it's A 7 5 U-T 9 0.*

19   How old did you say he was?
    *Eighty.*
    Only 18?

*No, eighty.*

20  What percentage of men would you say actually help with housework?
*Oh about 15 per cent.*
Did you say 50?
*No, fifteen.*

## Listening Exercise 2

*The purpose of this exercise is to give you practice in distinguishing voices from one another and identifying who is speaking. Listen to the six short conversations and answer the questions in your book for each conversation.*

**Note:** *There is no transcript for Listening exercise 2.*

## Listening Exercise 3

### STUDY STRATEGIES

I = Ira
E = Elizabeth

*Listen to this conversation and make notes of the useful strategies (in italics) for the Listening test that Elizabeth mentions.*

I   Elizabeth, You took the IELTS Test before going to university didn't you?
E   Yes, why?
I   Oh, I'm preparing for it at the moment.
E   How are you finding it?
I   Well, I'm having a few problems with the Listening. How can I get a good mark?
E   I'm sure you have heard this before but *the more you practice the better you'll do. Try to listen to as many different sources and accents as possible.*
I   I do that but my mind just goes blank when I take the test.
E   I know the problem. *One thing that helps is trying to use the questions to predict the answers before you listen.*
I   You mean *guess the answers?*
E   Yeah, and then listen to check your ideas. *Another thing to remember is that you can't lose marks if you're wrong so it is better to guess than leave a gap.*
I   But people on the tape speak so fast. I can't catch everything they say.
E   That's why it is so important to look at the questions before you listen. *Work out exactly what you are being asked; that way you can just listen for the answers rather than listening for every word.*
I   What do you mean?
E   For example, if the question starts 'how many' you know you are listening for a number, or if the question starts 'where' you know you are listening for a place.
I   So you don't need to concentrate on the bits in between?
E   No.
I   That sounds very easy but when do I get a chance to read all the questions?
E   *During the tape you get time to check your answers. Use some of this time to read ahead.*

I Apart from key words, is there anything else I should be looking for?

E *Diagrams, tables and charts give you a general outline and help you to understand the main topic of the conversation you are going to hear.*

I So in some ways reading is as important as listening.

E Yes, I suppose so, but *there are some clues on the tape itself, if you know how to listen for them. The speaker's intonation will often tell you when something important is going to be said. Also words like 'firstly' or 'moreover' give you some idea how the conversation is going to continue.*

I All this is very useful, but I still find that I don't really have enough time to answer all the questions.

E I had that problem as well. In the end *I found that I had to learn to write as I listened.*

I That's a good idea because at the moment I sometimes forget the answer before I have written it down.

E Is there anything else I can help you with?

I Not that I can think of at the moment, thank you very much.

## Practice Listening Test 2

*The question booklet for this test comes at the end of the Listening section. You may photocopy the booklet. In Section 1 you will hear a phone conversation of a man ordering items from a library. First, you will have some time to look at questions 1 to 6.*

**20 seconds**

*You will see that there is an example which has been done for you. On this occasion **only** the conversation relating to this will be played first.*

[phone rings]

Lib     Good morning, City Central Library. May I help you?

Man    Yes. I want to order some books and copies of articles please. You can send them to me through the post or courier, can't you?

Lib     Yes, certainly. I'll just get the form and take down some details. First your name please, sir.

Man    Lester Mackie. That's capital M, A-C-K-I-E.

*The man's name is Lester Mackie, so that is the name written on the form. Now we shall begin. You should answer the questions as you listen because you will not hear the recording a second time. First, you have another chance to look at questions 1 to 6.*

**10 seconds**

*Now listen carefully and answer questions 1 to 6*

[phone rings]

Lib     Good morning, City Central Library. May I help you?

Man    Yes. I want to order some books and copies of articles please. You can send them to me through the post or courier, can't you?

Lib     Yes, certainly. I'll just get the form and take down some details. First your name please, sir.

Man    Lester Mackie. That's capital M, A-C-K-I-E.

Lib     Mackie, Lester. And your membership number.

Man    That's M 9301274

Lib     M 9 3 0 …

Man    1 2 7 4.

| Lib | Thank you. Now your address please. That's the address you want us to send the items to. |
| Man | It's 17 Westmead Road, Annandale. |
| Lib | And could I have your phone number and your fax number please? |
| Man | Yes. The fax number is 863 5923. |
| Lib | 863 5? 923. |
| Man | That's correct. The daytime phone number is 02 579 6363 and after 5:00 p.m. it's 579 1857. |
| Lib | 579 1857. Thank you. And may I ask why you'll be needing the books? I'm sorry about this, but we have to have this information whenever we send books out from a telephone request. |
| Man | No problem. I'm preparing a short article for the environment watch section of the local newspaper. We're quite concerned about the problems we're facing here now, especially since we've been getting so many tourists in the district. |
| Lib | Oh I know. I'm so glad someone is doing something about publicising the problem. |
| Man | Now how long can I keep the books for? |
| Lib | Well as you know our normal loan period is three weeks with a two week extension over the phone. However, in cases where we send books out by post we allow a longer initial loan period to allow for the delivery time. So you may have the books for six weeks from the date of postage. But I'm afraid the two week extension won't apply then. However you would be able to renew them by bringing them in for stamping, provided no one else has a reserve on them. |
| Man | I should think the normal period will be enough. Now how do you prefer the postage and photocopy fees to be paid? |
| Lib | We accept both cash and credit card, but it will be such a small sum it might be more convenient to send us a money order. |
| Man | Hm. Would it be alright if I left it until I come in next time and just pay cash then? |
| Lib | Of course. There's no problem with that at all. |
| Man | Fine. I'll do that. Shall I tell you the articles I want copied first? |

*The man now tells the librarian the titles of the books and articles he wants. Look at questions 7 to 11, the titles of the books and mark each one according to whether it is available in the library, out on loan or will have to be requested from another library.*

**20 seconds**

*As you listen answer questions 7 to 11.*

| Lib | Good. I've got all that down. Now perhaps we could go on to the books. You tell me the books you need and I'll tell you whether we have them immediately available or whether you'll have to wait a bit for them, alright? The details I'll need are the author, the publication date and the title of the book. Is that OK? |
| Man | Yes no problem at all. Um, the first one is by Hallsworth, published in 1978. It's called *Land and Water Resources of Australia*. |
| Lib | Hm. Yes. We have that available on the shelves. |
| Man | Good. Now the next two are both government publications. The |

first one is rather old, published in 1984. That's *Land Degradation in Australia*, but the second one is more recent. That's *Coastal Zone Inquiry Report* from 1993.

**Lib**  I'm afraid we don't have the first one. We'd have to get that from the government archives for you, but the second one, the later one, has just come in so I'll put that aside for you.

**Man**  Wonderful. Now there are three more. Two rather old books, but they're standard works so you probably have them. *Environmental Law* by Fisher, and *Environmental Chemistry* by Raiswell. They were both published in 1980.

**Lib**  Ye-es we do have both those texts. *Environmental Law* should be on the shelf, but *Environmental Chemistry* is out on loan at the moment. I'll put that on reserve for you.

**Man**  Right. And the last one is *The Environmental Impact of Travel and Tourism* by M. Burns and Associates, 1989.

**Lib**  [slowly] Burns, M. *Environmental Impact* … No, I'm sorry we don't have that. I'll have to use the inter-library loan service and get it in for you.

**Man**  Oh. How long is that likely to take?

**Lib**  Well, it really depends where we can get it. If it's available locally it shouldn't take more than a few days but if we have to send overseas for it, it could be rather a while. We'll do our best to hurry it up.

*That is the end of Section 1. You now have half a minute to check your answers.*
**30 seconds**
*Now turn to Section 2. [pause] Section 2. You will hear a recording for a tour of the university library.*

*Look at the example on page 4 and at questions 12 to 16.*
**30 seconds**
*Answer questions 12 to 16 by writing the correct letters against the list of places.*
Welcome to the University of New South Wales library. This tour is a practical introduction to the library. It will take you to locations of services and materials without giving in-depth instruction. The tape itself runs for about 30 minutes. You may take as long as you need. Allow an hour to do a thorough tour of the library.

A brief explanation of the library structure is helpful before you begin your walk. The library occupies nine floors of the 14-storey main building, plus three floors of the adjoining Mathews building annex. This tour will cover floors one to nine and the three floors of the Mathews building annex, including general information and services.

You have commenced this tape at the general information desk on level two, where your tour begins. There are no book collections on this floor or on the first floor, which gives access to the library lawn. On this floor you find the Resource Centre for Disabled Users, Open Reserve, Unicopy and Loans and Returns. This means that you check out and return all books on this floor.

On floors three and four you will find the social sciences and humanities collections. You will also find the multimedia materials and the newspaper collection on floor three.

On the next three floors—that is, floors five, six and seven—we have the physical sciences library. However you should note that this does not include the biomedical library collection, which is located in the Mathews building annex. The entrance to the Mathews building annex is located on the third floor of this building and the biomedical collection occupies floors two, three and four of the annex.

The last two floors of the main building occupied by the library collection are floors eight and nine and here you will find the law library.

Now turn to your right and go towards the lifts.

*Before the final part of the talk, look at questions 17 to 21 on the general library information sheet on page 5 of your question booklet.*

**20 seconds**

*Now you will hear the rest of the talk. Answer questions 17 to 21.*

As you are walking towards the lifts, listen to this general information section of the recording. Please pay attention to the many signs throughout the library which give additional guidance. Pick up the yellow 'Finding Items in the Library' leaflet from the information desk if you do not have one already. This will assist you in understanding how material is arranged as you proceed on this tour.

Please note that eating, drinking and smoking are not allowed anywhere in the library building. Heed the warning that there is a high incidence of theft in the library. Never leave your belongings unattended. Telephones are on the first floor of the main building and there are clocks in all the lift lobbies.

As you will have realised by now, this university library is divided into four subject or special libraries; namely the biomedical library, social sciences and humanities library, physical sciences library and law library. Each special library provides a concentration of resources and services within their subject areas. As you proceed on this tour the special libraries will be explained to you in detail as you pass through each of them.

In front of you is a sign for women's toilets. From levels two to eight there are women's toilets on the even numbered floors, and the men's toilets are on the odd numbered floors near the lifts. Wheelchair access toilets are on levels one and two.

*That is the end of Section 2. You now have half a minute to check your answers.*

**30 seconds**

*Now turn to Section 3. [pause] Section 3. In this section you will hear Dr Richardson discussing the requirements of a course with a student. Listen to the discussion about the course requirements. As you listen, answer questions 22 to 31. First look at questions 22 to 29.*

**30 seconds**

*Now as you listen to the first part of the conversation, answer questions 22 to 29 [knocking on door]*

**Dr R**    Enter.

**St**    Good afternoon, Dr Richardson.

**Dr R**    Good afternoon. You're David Simmons, is that right?

**St**    Yes. I've an appointment to talk about the course requirements with you.

**Dr R**    Fine. Now why don't you take a seat over here and I'll just get some details from you. First, can I have your home address and your student number?

| St | That's 15 Market Avenue, Hornsby and my student number is C97H85. |
|---|---|
| Dr R | OK. Now I see here that you've already completed 18 credit points, but that you haven't done the Screen Studies course which is normally a pre-requisite for this course. Why is that David? |
| St | Oh, the course coordinator gave me an exemption because I've worked for a couple of years in the movie and television business and they considered my practical experience fulfilled the same requirements. |
| Dr R | Fine. Shall we go over the course requirements first, and then you can bring up any queries or problems you might have? It might be most useful to start with a few dates. The final examination will be in the last week of June, that's the week of the 23rd, but the final date hasn't been set; it should be the 25th or the 26th, but you don't have to worry about that yet. Before that, as you can see in your study guide, there are three essay assignments and some set exercises. I'll deal with these first. These set exercises are concerned with defining concepts and key terms. They do have fixed answers, not in the wording but in the content. To that extent they are quite mechanical, and provide an opportunity for you to do very well as long as your answers are very specific and clear. |
| St | Yes, I see there are about twenty terms here. How long should the answers be? |
| Dr R | You shouldn't exceed 250 words for each term. |
| St | Right, that looks easy enough. And the third assignment seems fairly straightforward too. Just a journalistic type review of a recent development in television. It's not so different to what I've done in my work. |
| Dr R | Yes, it should be fairly easy for you, but don't exceed 1000 words on that one. Essays 1 and 2 are the long ones. The first essay should be about 2000 words and the second 2500 to 3000, and the approach for both should be analytical. In the first your focus should be on TV and the audience and you should primarily consider the theoretical issues, particularly in relation to trying to understand audience studies. In the second, I'll want you to focus on analysing television programs. |
| St | Should I concentrate on one particular type of program for that? |
| Dr R | Not necessarily. But you must be careful not to overextend yourself here. A comparison between two programs or even between two channels is fine. Or a focus on one type of program, such as a particular series, works well here. |
| St | So if I wanted to look at television news programs, that would be OK? |
| Dr R | Yes, there'd be no problem with that. In fact it's quite a popular choice, and most students handle it very well. |
| St | Good. I'll probably do that, because it's the area I want to work in later. |

**10 seconds**

*Later during the course Dr Richardson gives David some advice and warnings about his essay.*

*Look at questions 30 and 31. As you listen answer questions 30 and 31.*
[knocking on door]

**Dr R**   Ah, come in and sit down David. You wanted to talk to me about your second essay, is that right?

**St**   Yes Dr Richardson. I just wanted your comments on what I'm planning to do. I'm doing the essay on the differences between TV news programs at different hours of the day.

**Dr R**   How many time slots were you planning to consider?

**St**   Well, I thought I'd look at all of them. That'd be 5 slots. The breakfast news, the mid-morning news and the midday news, that's three. Then there's the six o'clock, the ten o'clock and the midnight programs, so that's six, not five.

**Dr R**   Hm, that's rather a lot. And you'd have a lot of different audiences to consider. Why don't you just do two, say the mid-morning and the six o'clock? That should give you two fairly contrasting approaches with two main audience compositions.

**St**   Oh, just two then?

**Dr R**   Yes, I think that'd be much better. Now how many actual programs do you plan to work with?

**St**   I suppose you think analysing a whole week of news programs would be too many?

**Dr R**   Well that depends on how much of each program. If you concentrate on one particular type of news item, say the sports news or local items it might be alright.

**St**   Yes, I can see that would be a good idea. I won't make a decision now, before I collect a sample of programs over a whole week. I'll look at them and see what items appear throughout the week.

**Dr R**   Yes, that's a sound approach. Now we're getting close to the deadline. Can you finish in time?

**St**   Yes, I think so. I've completed the reading and I know what my basic approach is, so it's really just a matter of pulling it all together now.

**Dr R**   Fine, David. I'll look forward to reading it.

*That is the end of Section 3. You will now have half a minute to check your answers*
   **30 seconds**

*Now turn to Section 4.* [pause] *Section 4. In this section you will hear a lecture about coastal environmental problems. First read the summary of the lecture made by a student and look at questions 32 to 40*
   **20 seconds**

*As you listen complete the summary. Use no more than three words for each answer. The first one has been done for you as an example.*

Good afternoon everyone. Today we have with us Mr Kevin Ackroyd, a representative from the Department of the Environment to outline the results of last year's inquiry into environmental problems along the coastline. Mr Ackroyd.

Thank you Ms Cranston. Good afternoon everyone. Perhaps it would be best if I first outline for you what I plan to talk about. I'll begin with some background to the inquiry looking at the new demands we are making on our old resources, so to speak, and then go on to give you some idea of the conclusions we came to in our inquiry.

OK, first the background. The inquiry was sparked off because various concerned residents in the coastal region realised that the recent population shift, which really got going in the 1970s, was putting extreme pressure on our coastal environment. Over the past two decades half of the country's population growth has been in the non-metropolitan areas. Today, nine out of ten people live in the coastal zone.

The reasons for this shift are not yet fully understood, but there is a range of factors which probably contribute, including economic development, an ageing population, and growth in industry, particularly tourism and its associated industries. We would have to admit that government policies have also contributed to this trend. A trend which is likely to continue so that it's estimated that by the year 2000 there will be a million additional people living in the non-metropolitan coastal zone. This population expansion puts considerable pressure on the natural resources of the zone, and there are two factors likely to impose particular strains. These are firstly that those areas of greatest growth in the past are likely to continue to grow as strongly as before—in other words, urban sprawl or expansion will continue for at least another decade. The second factor contributing to the pressure is industry, particularly the newer industries like tourism. These newer industries will compete for resources with other users such as the intensive fish and shellfish farming industry.

All of this will take place in an environment that is already under severe stress, and in particular the water resources will be degraded. It is the view of the inquiry that water degradation, whether of seas, rivers or lakes, is the greatest resource problem in the coastal zone as a whole.

*[pause of 5 seconds]*

Now the conclusions of the inquiry can be stated quite plainly and simply. First we must raise the profile of the coastal zone in our thinking, especially in our approach to conservation and economic development.

Second, we must exercise much greater vision. We must be prepared to think in the long term rather than the short term, and to pay attention to detail; so, better management and better planning.

And thirdly we must adopt a *national* approach. We can no longer afford to leave the decision making to individual departments, to local government bodies or even to the central government. We are looking here at the need for coordination on a *nationwide* level. To achieve workable, effective results involving all levels of government as well as the various non-government organisations in this country will be no easy task, but it is imperative we try.

Well, I see time is running out, so perhaps if I just summarise the recommendations made by the inquiry for you:

- the long view prevails over the short
- broad considerations predominate over narrow
- the techniques of modern management, and the tools of modern economics are brought into operation
- people being affected by decisions (including indigenous people) are adequately consulted before decisions are made.

With that I'll stop and give you the opportunity to ask a few questions. But perhaps first I should tell you that the full report of the inquiry *[fade out]* is available from the GPS, the Government Publishing Service.

*That is the end of the Listening test. You will now have half a minute to check your answers*

*30 seconds*

*You now have ten minutes to transfer your answers to the Listening answer sheet.*

## Practice Listening Test 3

*The question booklet for this test is at the end of the Listening section. You may photocopy this booklet. In Section 1 you will hear two people talking about the towns where they grew up. First, you will have some time to look at questions 1 to 9.*

**20 seconds**

*You will see that there is an example which has been done for you. On this occasion only, the conversation relating to this will be played first.*

**Maureen** Time goes so quickly—I can't believe that I will have been here for five years on Saturday.

**Gordon** That's a long time. Where did you live before that?

**Maureen** I lived in a small town, about 150 miles from Perth, on the southwest coast of Australia, called Albany.

**Gordon** When you say 'small', how small do you mean?

**Maureen** Oh around 12 000 people.

**Gordon** What is it like growing up somewhere that small?

*Now we shall begin. You should answer the questions as you listen because you will not hear the recording a second time. First, you have another chance to look at questions 1 to 3.*

**10 seconds**

*Listen carefully and answer questions 1 to 3.*

**Maureen** Time goes so quickly—I can't believe that I will have been here for five years on Saturday.

**Gordon** That's a long time. Where did you live before that?

**Maureen** I lived in a small town, about 150 miles from Perth, on the southwest coast of Australia, called Albany.

**Gordon** When you say 'small', how small do you mean?

**Maureen** Oh around 12 000 people.

**Gordon** What is it like growing up somewhere that small?

**Maureen** Well, It has advantages. People tend to be much more friendly in small towns. You seem to get to know more people. The pace of life is much slower, everyone seems to have more time to talk and generally the lifestyle is much more relaxed. On the other hand, small-town life can be pretty boring. Obviously, you haven't got the same range of entertainments available as in the city, and unless you want to go into farming you have to move elsewhere to look for a job.

**Gordon** So farming is the main industry then?

**Maureen** Well, actually, no. There is a lot of sheep and cattle farming and more recently a lot of people have started to grow potatoes. However, the town was first established as a whaling base and although there isn't any whaling today, most people are still employed by the fishing industry.

**Gordon** What's the weather like?

**Maureen** In summer you get some fairly nice days, but it gets very windy.

|          | In winter, I guess the average temperature is about 15 degrees Celsius, and it gets really windy and it's very, very wet. |
| **Gordon** | Sounds lovely, I can see why you are here. |
| **Maureen** | Oh come on, it's not all that bad. It's got a beautiful coastline, and beautiful beaches. You can drive for about 45 minutes and you will come to absolutely deserted white beaches. You can be the only person swimming there. |
| **Gordon** | With that wind I'm not surprised! |
| **Maureen** | Don't be like that, we do get some good days. Anyway, where do you come from? |

*Maureen goes on to ask Gordon about his home town. Look at questions 4 to 9.*

**20 seconds**

*Write the answers to questions 4 to 9.*

|          |          |
| **Gordon** | I come from a town called Watford, about 17 miles from the centre of London. |
| **Maureen** | Is it a big town? |
| **Gordon** | Not really, It has a population of around 80–90 000 but the whole area is built up so it is hard to say where Watford finishes and the other towns begin. |
| **Maureen** | Did you enjoy living there? |
| **Gordon** | Well, being so close to London has advantages. You get the latest films and music. There is always something going on and there is such a wide variety of different people and cultures that it is difficult to get bored. Of course all this has its downside—the cost of living is very expensive and most people cannot afford to go out very often. So although the entertainment is available you have to have a lot of money to enjoy it. Another problem is like most big cities there is a lot of crime and there are areas of London that are very dangerous. |
| **Maureen** | What are the main industries in Watford? |
| **Gordon** | Of course a lot of people commute into London but there is also a lot of local industry. Before desktop publishing, Watford used to be the centre of the printing industry in Britain. Also, there used to be a big factory manufacturing helicopter engines but that closed down about two years ago. Nowadays the biggest industries are electronics and light engineering. |
| **Maureen** | I suppose that it gets a lot of snow being in England? |
| **Gordon** | Not really. It usually snows once a year and it rarely lasts for more than two or three days. The weather is mainly cold and wet. Sometimes you get a light rain that lasts for weeks. |
| **Maureen** | Is there anything you miss particularly about living there? |
| **Gordon** | Near my parents' house there is a large park. I suppose it is about 10 square miles in size and it has a canal and a river running through the middle of it. There are some nice walks, you can go fishing and there are good sports facilities. Sometimes I miss that. |
| **Maureen** | Would you like to go back? |
| **Gordon** | I don't know, I'm quite happy here at the moment. I like the weather. It's great to get up in the morning and know that it is going to be sunny. What about you? |

| **Maureen** | Probably but not for a long time yet. At the moment I enjoy the excitement of the city. My work and most of my friends are here and it is nice to know that there are so many facilities available. However, I think that Albany might be a good place to retire. It's safe and it's easy to make friends there. |
| **Gordon** | I'm going to be here for a while too. I have just signed a new contract for my job which means that I'll be living here for at least another five years. |

*That is the end of Section 1. You now have half a minute to check your answers.*
**30 seconds**
*Turn to Section 2 on page 3 of your question booklet. [pause] Section 2. You will hear a presenter giving information about the site of an art and music festival. Look at questions 10 to 14 and the map.*
**20 seconds**
*As you listen write the appropriate letter from the map next to the facilities stated in questions 10 to 12 and write down the answers for questions 13 and 14.*
Good Afternoon, I'd just like to make a few announcements before the first performances begin at this year's Hetherington Art and Music Festival.

Firstly, a short guide to some of the more important places on the site. There are three stages. Stage 1 is the main stage and is where I am speaking from now. Stages 2 and 3 are opposite each other to the left and right of the main stage. The first aid post is located directly behind me and to the northeast of the main stage. The organiser's office is next to the rear entrance and this is where lost children can be reunited with their parents. In front of this office you will find ten public telephones. These telephones can only be used to telephone out; they will not receive incoming calls. Toilets are to be found in all four corners of the stadium site. If you lose anything you should make a report at the security post next to stage 2. Remember to visit the souvenir stalls in the car park in front of the main entrance to the stadium.

If you want to leave the stadium for any reason, please remember to keep your ticket with you, as you will not be readmitted without it. While on this subject, to make exit and re-entry simpler, could everyone leaving the site use the main entrance at the other side of the car park leading to Gladstone Road. This is to allow performers easy access to the site through the rear gate behind the main stage. Most importantly, when leaving the area of the stadium try to keep as quiet as possible so as not to disturb our neighbours. We have already been warned that we will not be given permission to hold the festival next year if there are complaints from local residents.
*Now the presenter goes on to explain the evening's schedule. Look at the entertainment program and questions 15 to 19.*
**20 seconds**
*Answer questions 15 to 19 to complete the table.*
Now that I've got the official announcements out of the way, I'd like to tell you about tonight's program. The Brazilian Drum Band will be appearing on stage 3 at 7.00. This is the first time that they have performed outside South America, so their show is not to be missed. This will be followed by Claude and Jacques, the French mime artists, at around 8.00. During the performance Claude and Jacques will be introducing special guests from the fields of music and dance. Meanwhile, on stage 2, there is a modern ballet from Great Grapefruit Incorporated, illustrating women's role in world peace. This will

begin at 7.00 and last for roughly 2 hours. Stage 1 begins at 9.00 with the jazz fusion band, Crossed Wires, whose performance tonight is the last date on their world tour. Stage 1 continues with a regular guest at these festivals, comedian Tom Cobble. His show begins at 10.30.

After Claude and Jacques at 9.00 on stage 3, there will be a performance by the Flying Barito Brothers who are acrobats with the Albanian State Circus. The Flying Barito Brothers' fire-eating trapeze act is unique. No other performer has managed to equal their grand finale. From 11.15 we are happy to present Winston Smiles and the Kingston Beat who will be playing authentic Jamaican reggae until the end of the official program at 1.30.

Over on stage 2, the Great Mysteron will be presenting his show of magic illusion and mystery at 9.30. During the show he will be chained and thrown into a sealed aquarium from which he will try to escape. If everything goes to plan the act will finish at 11.30 and the stage will be ready for the country and western music of Blue Grass Ben and the Cattlemen at 12.00. This act will be the last on stage 2 tonight.

After Tom Cobble on stage 1, we have tonight's main attraction The Proffets, who will be performing in public tonight for the first time since they broke up 5 years ago. The news is that they are back and they will be presenting a show including both old favourites and songs from their new album, which is to be released in September. They are expected on stage at midnight. After the official program has ended there will be a number of side shows taking place around the site.

*That is the end of Section 2. You will now have half a minute to check your answers*
**30 seconds**
Turn to Section 3 on page 5 of your question booklet. [pause] Section 3. You will hear two students discussing a survey they have to write as an assignment. Look at questions 20–25.
**30 seconds**
Now listen and complete questions 20 to 25.

**Theresa** How is your market research project going, Frank?

**Frank** Very well actually, Theresa. I have just got the results of the survey back and so now I have got to draw some conclusions from the information I've collected.

**Theresa** That's good. I'm still writing my questionnaire. In fact I'm starting to panic as the project deadline is in two weeks and I don't seem to be making any progress at all.

**Frank** What is your topic?

**Theresa** Forms of transportation in the city. What about you?

**Frank** I've been finding out people's attitudes to the amount of violence on television.

**Theresa** That's interesting. What do your results show?

**Frank** Well, as I said I haven't finished writing my conclusions yet, but it seems most people think there is a problem. Unfortunately, there is no real agreement on the action that needs to be taken. Nearly everyone surveyed said that there was too much violence on TV. A lot of people complained that American police serials and Chinese Kung Fu films were particularly violent. The main objection seems to be that although a lot of people get shot, stabbed, decapitated and so on, the films never show the consequences of this violence. Although people die and get horribly injured, nobody seems to suffer or live with the injuries. Any children watching might take the heroes of these programs as role models and copy their behaviour.

**Theresa** So what did most people suggest should be done?

**Frank** A lot of people are concerned about how these films affect children. They are particularly worried that children will try to behave like the stars. The survey shows that violent programs should only be broadcast after 10.00 p.m. when most children are already in bed. There is also a significant minority of people who feel that violent films should be banned altogether.

**Theresa** How did people feel about the violence on news broadcasts?

**Frank** Most of the responses I have looked at have felt that violence on news broadcasts is more acceptable as it's real. Although it is unpleasant, it is important to keep in touch with reality. Still, many people thought that it would be better to restrict violent scenes to late evening.

*Frank and Theresa discuss the methods they are using to conduct their surveys. Look at questions 26 to 29.*

**30 seconds**

*Listen and complete questions 26 to 29.*

**Theresa** Your survey sounds very good. How many people filled it in?

**Frank** I gave out 120 copies and I got 70 back.

**Theresa** That's a very high rate of return. Who did you give your questionnaires to?

**Frank** I gave a copy to every student in my hall of residence and a few to friends from other colleges.

**Theresa** Don't you think that this will influence your results?

**Frank** How do you mean?

**Theresa** The people in your hall of residence will all be about the same age. They are all students, most of them studying similar subjects and from similar backgrounds. Therefore it is likely that they will have similar opinions. Your results represent student opinion not public opinion.

**Frank** So how are you going to do your research?

**Theresa** I'm going to interview my respondents in the shopping mall. What I'll do is ask people if they have five minutes to spare to answer a few questions. If they agree I will ask them some multiple choice questions and tick off their answers on my sheet. That way I can select people of all ages and attitudes, so my sample should be reasonably representative.

**Frank** Isn't it very difficult to ask meaningful questions using multiple choice?

**Theresa** Yes, it is. I suppose your survey has the advantage of more detailed information. However, in most cases people won't bother to give answers that require too much effort on their part. The secret to writing a successful survey is to write simple multiple choice questions that target the information you are looking for. Therefore, it is better to write a lot of short specific questions than longer general ones.

**Frank** So that's why it is taking you so long to write.

**Theresa** Yeah, but I hope I will be ready to start interviewing at the weekend.

*That is the end of Section 3. You now have half a minute to check your answers.*
**30 seconds**
*Now turn to Section 4 on page 7 of your question booklet. [pause] Section 4. You will hear a lecturer giving a lecture on quality control. Read a summary of the lecture made by a student and look at questions 30–35.*
**30 seconds**
*Now listen to the lecture and answer questions 30–35.*

Good morning ladies and gentleman. Today's topic in our series of lectures on the stages of the production process is quality control. Some people believe that an effective quality control system amounts to an inspection of the finished product. This morning I intend to prove to you why those people are mistaken.

The main drawback with a finished product inspection is that it is 'an after the act' operation. No amount of inspection can make bad work good. For this reason most large-scale manufacturers consider quality control to be an ongoing process. The advantages of this are considerable. It cuts wastage, it saves time, as no hours are lost on work done on already defective items, and perhaps most importantly it is easier to detect a fault, when the product is still at the component stage.

So when should quality control begin? Well, usually with the raw materials. If the materials are of sub-standard quality there is no point in processing them. More to the point, sub-standard materials can be returned to the company at no cost to the manufacturer. Although these benefits seem obvious, you might be surprised to know that only 87 per cent of large firms and 62 per cent of small firms have a standard raw material inspection procedure. For the same reasons it is a good idea to test components brought in from another company.

In many manufacturing processes it is useful to carry out some form of quality control on products while they are still being manufactured. It is often easier to check individual components before assembly takes place. Equally, it may be valuable to test components by their function. I suppose the bottom line is that every product and every company has its own requirements and the quality control program should be arranged accordingly.

The next question that needs to be asked is 'what are we testing for?' Again this depends on the product. An expensive car has different requirements from a cheap plastic toy. However, in both cases the most vital testing is for safety.

An increasingly common reason for testing these days is environmental impact. As the public becomes more and more concerned about green issues, it is becoming more and more important to measure a product's effect on the environment. This testing must assess the impact of both the product itself and the manufacturing process.

*Questions 36 to 40. Before the final part of the lecture look at questions 36 to 40.*
**30 seconds**
*Answer questions 36 to 40 according to the information given in the lecture.*

This brings me to my next point—standards. Of course standards imposed vary greatly from country to country and industry to industry. However, 87 per cent of all companies in Australia do have written quality controls set out; 80

per cent of these are developed within the firm. These standards are nearly always based on guidelines set out by one of the major control boards. Sixty-five per cent of these companies have adopted standards in line with SAA (Standards Association of Australia), while a further 22 per cent use standards set up by individual trade or industry associations. Only 23 per cent of firms have a set of standards which adhere to international requirements. This 23 per cent represents some of Australia's major exporters.

So, who is responsible for quality control? Well again there is no one answer. Companies place different levels of importance on quality control. A recent survey tried to find out who usually takes charge of the quality control function. It was discovered that 18 per cent of top management were directly responsible. While 56 per cent of middle management and 26 per cent of quality control personnel oversaw this function within their company. It seems that most manufacturing industries see quality control as a middle management task.

The final thing I want to do this morning is to consider the effect of releasing undetected low-quality items. The manufacturer stands to lose a great deal:

- through direct loss of custom
- through possible further loss of custom and goodwill when 'word gets around' that the quality standard is unreliable
- through the cost of dealing with and compensating the customer who has complained
- through the need to maintain higher replacement stocks and a large repair force.

In conclusion, quality control is a vital part of the manufacturing process, helping to ensure that Australian products remain competitive in the market place.

*That is the end of the Listening test. You will now have half a minute to check your answers.*

**30 seconds**
*You now have ten minutes to transfer your answers to the Listening answer sheet.*

# Speaking Transcripts

## Practice Interview 1

*For this exercise you should listen to the interviewer's questions. Then, when you hear the beep, stop your cassette and reply to the questions. When you have finished speaking start your cassette again.*

Good Morning. Could you tell me your name and candidate number please?

And what would you like me to call you?

Tell me a bit about your family.

What do your brothers and sisters do?

So, where are you from?

What are the advantages and disadvantages of living here?

I'm new here. Could you recommend a good restaurant?

Why do you like it?

What type of food does it serve?

What do you suggest I order?

Is it expensive?

How do I get there?

After you have taken the IELTS, what are you planning to study?
Why are you interested in this?

Why do you want to study overseas?

### SAMPLE TASK 3

Now what I want to do is something a bit different. I want you to ask me some questions. This morning I saw an accident and I would like you to ask me some questions to find out what happened. Here is a card with some ideas to help you. Read the card and start when you are ready.

It happened at about 7.30 this morning.

I was reading the newspaper in the train.

The train crashed into a truck on a level crossing.

The accident took place just out of town.

There were 12 people injured.

The truck broke down on the level crossing and the train couldn't stop in time.

OK, good. I would like to go back to you now. How do you think studying overseas will be different to studying in your own country?

So what problems do you think you will have studying abroad?

Do you think you will have many difficulties adapting to a new culture?

Do you think that there will be any major changes in your field of study over the next few years?

How do you think an overseas degree will improve your professional skills?

What do you intend to do once you have finished your studies?

What do you see yourself doing professionally in 10 years' time?

And how do you see your personal life changing?

OK. I think that's is all I want to ask you today. Thank you very much. It was very interesting talking to you and I wish you all the best with your future studies. Goodbye now.

## Practice Interview 2

*For this exercise you should listen to the interviewer's questions. Then when you hear the beep, stop your cassette and reply to the questions. When you have finished speaking start your cassette again.*

Good afternoon. My name is Katherine Pollock. Could I have your name please?

And your candidate number?

Thank you. Now could you tell me a little about yourself?

And where do you live?

What kind of place is that? For example, is it a city? An industrial area?

What are some of the nicest things about where you live?

Are there any places of special interest I could visit in your home area?

Could you describe some of them for me?

What would be the best way for me to get there?

What sort of places could I stay at?

Should I go at any special time of year?

I see. This has all been very interesting.

### SAMPLE TASK 4

Now I want to change the interview so that you can ask me some questions. I have some visitors from overseas and I want you to ask me about them. Here is a card with some suggestions of things for you to find out.

Two young women. Michiko and Raquel.

They're from Brazil.

We were studying together in America.

They'll be here for about three weeks.

We'll take a trip to the mountains, and probably go to the coast for a weekend also.

We'll certainly go to lots of films and restaurants, and perhaps a disco or two.

Thank you. That was very good.

Now let's go back to real life and you. Tell me, what do you think are the greatest problems facing your country at present?

And what has been done so far to solve these problems?

How successful would you say these measures have been?

Do you think things are likely to get better or worse in the future?

Is what you are going to study likely to be of use in helping solve these problems do you think?

Thank you very much. It's been pleasant talking to you. I wish you success in your study program. Goodbye.

# Appendix

**Note:** *Words in parenthesis () may be included in the answer but are not essential to score a mark. A slash between words or phrases indicates alternative answers. For example, 'people argue/disagree' means both 'people argue' and 'people disagree' are correct answers. When the Answer Key indicates two or three letters (e.g. C D E) you must have **all** to be correct.*

# Answer Key

## Prediction

1 **C** Horror films are usually shown late at night.
Cookery programs and the Open University are not usually shown at peak hours.
In most countries 7.00 p.m. would be a popular time for a news broadcast.

2 **A** The buffet at the Hilton would be too expensive for students.
Roast beef takes a long time to cook so it would have to be planned.
Cornflakes are eaten in the morning.

3 **B** No one *has* to watch a football match.
Malcolm's lecturer would not like to hear from him in the evening.
The telephone office is unlikely to be open.

4 **A** Being worried about losing your money is not an excuse for not going out.
Sheila would probably have to go out to borrow some money.
If Sheila has borrowed some money she can go out.

5 **A** Not being tired is not a decision.
If Malcolm has an exam the next morning he should go to bed.
There is no other mention of a party.

6      River. Only rivers have banks that burst.

7      The answer has to be a number of days.

8      Missing. The report has already mentioned the number of dead and injured.

9      If the area is under water the only form of transport would be by boat.

10     Flooded. Runways are on the ground and so likely to be flooded.

11–12 **A C** There is obviously no risk of fire. Food and money are not immediate needs in this kind of situation.

## Practice Listening Test 1

### SECTION 1

Questions 1–6
1  D
2  B
3  C
4  D
5  C  D
6  A  E
7  7

Questions 8–11. *The sequence is not relevant, as long as the letter matches the activity.*
8  A  boating
9  C  cliff walks
10  E  swimming
11  F  bird watching

### SECTION 2

Questions 12–17
12  (almost) one/a million
13  60%/600 000
14  one in five/20%/200 000

Questions 15–16. *Any sequence*
15  joyriders
16  professionals
17  professional
18  B
19  C

### SECTION 3

Questions 20–29
20  too much
21  new words
22  getting own ideas
23  too many / too early / not enough time
24  boring / not interesting
25  interesting / get(s) (most) benefit(s) / new information
26  give / giving presentations / reading seminar papers
27  people argue / disagree
28  D
29  B

### SECTION 4

Questions 30–35. *Any sequence.*
30  study guide
31  course reader
32  university book shop
33  more difficult than / more challenging than
34  understanding of cultures / cross-cultural sensitivity / understanding
35  cultural history

Questions 36–37. *Any sequence.*
36  India / Indian
37  China / Chinese
38  cultural / religious / trade / trading
39  links / connections
40  background / basis / base

### THERE IS NO ANSWER KEY TO LISTENING EXERCISE 1

Check your answers to this exercise against the transcript (page 74).

## Listening Exercise 2

| Conversation 1 | Conversation 2 |
|---|---|
| Greg | Wendy |
| Bruce | Barbara |
| Bruce | Wendy |
| Greg | Barbara |

| Conversation 3 | Conversation 4 |
|---|---|
| Suzanne | Jeremy |
| Carolyn | Jeremy |
| Suzanne | Colin |
|  | Colin |

| Conversation 5 | Conversation 6 |
|---|---|
| Arthur | Kathy |
| David | Alison |
| David | Alison |
| David | Kathy |
| Arthur |  |

Check your notes to this exercise against the transcript (page 75).

## Practice Listening Test 2

### SECTION 1

*Questions 1–11*
1  M 9301274
2  863 5923
3  579 1857
4  B
5  B
6  D
7  R
8  A
9  A
10  OL
11  R

### SECTION 2

*Questions 12–21*
12  H
13  F G
14  G
15  C D E
16  J K L
17  lift lobbies
18  subject libraries / special libraries / specialist libraries
19  even [number(ed)]
20  odd [number(ed)]
21  one (&) two / 1 (&) 2

### SECTION 3

*Questions 22–31*
22  ~~9307568~~  C97H85
23  (has/given) exemption / (has) practical experience / TV/film/movie experience
24  25, 26 June
25  C
26  B
27  M
28  T A
29  J
30  A
31  collect a sample / collect sample programs

### SECTION 4

*Questions 32–40*
32  coastal environment / environment of coast / natural resources / water resources
33  population shift / urban expansion / population growth / expansion
34  ageing population
35  government policies
36  urban sprawl / urban expansion / growth will continue
37  (intensive) fish / (intensive) shellfish / (intensive) fish, shellfish
38  adopt national approach / nationwide coordination
39  management and economics / management, economic practices
40  people affected / people concerned

## Practice Listening Test 3

### SECTION 1

*Questions 1–9*
1  12 000 / 12 thousand
2  boring / no entertainment
3  fishing
4  cost of living / expensive
5  cold and wet
6  (large) park
7  the weather
8  when she retires
9  5 years

### SECTION 2

*Questions 10–19*
10  E
11  D
12  B
13  keep/have your ticket
14  complaints
15  (modern) ballet
16  9.00
17  3
18  11.15
19  country and western

## Section 3

Questions 20–29
20  C
21  B
22  B
23  role models
24  (significant) minority
25  reality / real (life)
26  70
27  public opinion
28  (the) shopping mall
29  short (and) specific / multiple choice / simple

## Section 4

Questions 30–40
30  bad work good
31  (it) cuts wastage
32  (it) saves time
33  62%
34  safety
35  (the) manufacturing process
36  C
37  B
38  A
39  B or D
40  D or B

## True Or False Exercise

1  **False.** The interview is not a grammar test although grammar is one of the factors taken into account when giving a band score.

2  **True.** If you memorise your answers you will find it very difficult to answer questions you haven't predicted. Also, the interviewer will give you a lower band score if he or she thinks you have rehearsed.

3  **False.** You are assessed on your overall fluency so a few grammar errors will not significantly effect your score. Besides, in an ordinary conversation small grammatical errors will often go undetected.

4  **False.** It is impossible to know exactly what you are going to say before the interview because you don't know the questions you will be asked. However, this is not to say that you shouldn't think about topics that might arise during the interview.

5  **True.** As long as you keep to the question, the longer and more detailed the answer, the better. The interviewer will change the topic when he or she feels it is necessary.

6  **False.** The questions will almost always be different.

7  **False.** Usually the interviewer will be responsible for your band score.

8  **True.** It is you who is being tested, so it is your life and plans that are of interest. This is particularly true during Phase 3, when you should restrict your questions to the subject of the elicitation.

9  **True.** In the official IELTS handbook it says that: 'assessment takes into account evidence of communicative strategies and appropriate and flexible use of grammar and vocabulary'.

10  It depends on the person. Different people find different sections of the test easier or more difficult.

# LISTENING ANSWER SHEET

| | | |
|---|---|---|
| 1 | | |
| 2 | | |
| 3 | | |
| 4 | | |
| 5 | | |
| 6 | | |
| 7 | | |
| 8 | | |
| 9 | | |
| 10 | | |
| 11 | | |
| 12 | | |
| 13 | | |
| 14 | | |
| 15 | | |
| 16 | | |
| 17 | | |
| 18 | | |
| 19 | | |
| 20 | | |
| 21 | | |
| | | |

| | | |
|---|---|---|
| 22 | | |
| 23 | | |
| 24 | | |
| 25 | | |
| 26 | | |
| 27 | | |
| 28 | | |
| 29 | | |
| 30 | | |
| 31 | | |
| 32 | | |
| 33 | | |
| 34 | | |
| 35 | | |
| 36 | | |
| 37 | | |
| 38 | | |
| 39 | | |
| 40 | | |
| 41 | | |
| 42 | | |
| Listening total | | |

# SPEAKING TEST
## PERSONAL DETAILS

*These are the details you will have to fill in for the IELTS Speaking test.*

Family name:_____

Other names:_____

Nationality: _____

First language:_____

Occupation: _____

Work experience:_____

_____

_____

_____

How did you learn English?_____

_____

_____

_____

What are your personal interests?_____

_____

_____

_____

What are your future plans?_____

_____

_____

_____

Why are you taking this test?_____

_____

_____

_____

## ASSESSMENT

## FOR EXAMINER'S USE

# Acknowledgments

The authors wish to thank the following people.

For technical assistance: Edy L. Alting and Itje Simon.

Voices: Angela Black, David Casson-Medhurst, Joanna Crichton, Geoffrey Crewes, Robert C. Currie, Kathy Howard, Richard L. Howells, Victoria Markwick-Smith, B. A. Quealy, Carolyn Ritchie, Mark Roberts, Arthur Rush, Tetty Simanjuntak, Alisson P. Spice, Richard Stewart and Barbara Wiechecki.

Greg Clough, Colin Pantal, Nigel Vickers, Asjik Mubanar, David Airth and Suzanne Fegan.